Struggling for Nation Building

A Brief History of All India Bank Officers' Confederation

Sarika Chaudhary
Archana Prasad

AAKAR

Struggling for Nation Building
Sarika Chaudhary and Archana Prasad

First Published 2018

ISBN 978-93-5002-573-4

Published by
AAKAR BOOKS
28 E Pocket IV, Mayur Vihar Phase I
Delhi 110 091
aakarbooks@gmail.com
www.aakarbooks.com

Designed by
Limited Colors, Delhi 110 092

Printed at
Sapra Brothers, Noida

Foreword

A long cherished dream has come true. The younger generations can now get a glimpse of the history of the unique managerial class confederation, the All India Bank Officers' Confederation (AIBOC). The AIBOC's struggles have been exemplary for an officers' organization. The struggles were not only for securing rights and improving service conditions but also gave equal importance to the struggles for nation building. These struggles were for preserving our unity in diversity, protecting the public sector character of the banks, examining the policies of the government, safeguarding social banking, and keeping lending policies accessible for the larger masses.

The AIBOC could achieve many of these due to the formation of the United Forum of Bank Unions (UFBU), which is again a unique organisation. There are differences within the UFBU but these are kept aside for a common cause. It is because of the UFBU that even after 27 years of repeated attempts at privatization by different governments, no public sector bank has been privatized.

Similarly, the court cases fought by the AIBOC, a recourse that is attempted only when other options for struggle have been tried, have proved to be of great achievements. It is not possible to cover the entire history of the AIBOC within these pages, but what we witness herein are glimpses. These should motivate every affiliates to write their own history. The efforts of Sarika Chaudhary and Archana Prasad require admiration and acknowledgement.

Aakar Books have to be thanked for taking up the publication in a record time.

My only appeal to our officers, employees, trade unionists and the public at large is to read this book. It will prove to be a source of strength to the people's and trade union movements.

D. Thomas Franco Rajendra Dev
General Secretary, AIBOC
Secretary General, AIPCOC
ngcfranco@gmail.com

Contents

Acknowledgements

We would like to express our special thanks to D. Thomas Franco Rajendra Dev for entrusting us the opportunity to write the history of the All India Bank Officers' Confederation. Without his support and direction, this project could not have been possible. The whole team of the AIBOC has been most supportive in this project. They provided us with all the required documents and arranged the logistics for the research in this project.

The interviews taken for this project were very helpful in shaping our understanding about the history of the AIBOC. A special thanks is due to L.V. Subramaniam, who provided us with his precious time and illuminated us regarding the initial struggles of the bank officers. Also, the two interviews with Shantha Raju gave a broad idea not just about the officers' and award staff's struggles but also the problems faced by the whole banking sector from the time of the colonial rule till date. The interviews provided by the previous General Secretaries and Presidents of the AIBOC like Shantha Raju, G.D. Nadaf, Harvinder Singh, A.K. Jana, P.K. Sarkar and Y. Sudarshan were very helpful. The support and assistance of other leaders of the AIBOC like K.V. Acharya, Deepak K. Basu, Suprita Sarker, T.N. Goel among others also deserves our thanks.

A special mention is due to V. Rajani, Nagaraja Shastry and Sudhanshu Mukharjee without whom access to the documents used in this study and interviews with its leaders would not have been possible. We thank Soumya Dutta for providing us with all the arrangements required for the work at our Kolkata visit. Suraj Telange for providing comments on the first draft, for which he deserves our thanks. And we would also like to thank Aakar Books for publishing the book in such a short time period.

A special thanks needs to be given to Saket Moon, Dinesh Abrol and Praveen Jha for their support to this project. Comments and conversations with them were very useful in developing ideas.

This book is dedicated to all the struggling comrades of the All India Bank Officers' Confederation.

Sarika Chaudhary
Archana Prasad

List of Acronyms

AIABOF	All India Andhra Bank Officers' Federation
AIWCCPI	All India Average Working Class Consumer Price Index
AIBEA	All India Bank Employees' Association
AIBOBOF	All India Bank of Baroda Officers' Federation
AIBOA	All India Bank Officers' Association
AIBOC	All India Bank Officers' Confederation
AICOBOO	All India Confederation of Bank Officers' Organisations
AINBOF	All India Nationalised Banks Officers' Federation
AIPSBOF	All India Private Sector Banks Officers' Federation
AIRRBOF	All India Regional Rural Bank Officers' Federation
AISBISF	All India State Bank of India Staff Federation
AISBOF	All India State Bank Officers' Federation
AITUC	All India Trade Union Congress
CCA	City Compensatory Allowance
CPI(M)	Communist Party of India (Marxist)
DA/D.A.	Dearness Allowance
DRTs	Debt Recovery Tribunals

E.C.	Executive Committee
FRDI	Financial Resolution and Deposit Insurance
FDI	Foreign Direct Investments
H.R.A/HRA	House Rent Allowance
IBA	Indian Banks' Association
INBOC	Indian National Bank Officers' Congress
IDBI	Industrial Development Bank of India
JAC	Joint Action Committee
LIC	Life Insurance Corporation
NABARD	National Bank for Agriculture and Rural Development
PCR	Pillai Committee Recommendations
NPAs	Non-performing assets
PWTUC	Professional Workers' Trade Union Centre of India
RRB	Regional Rural Bank
RBI	Reserve Bank of India
SBI	State Bank of India
UFBU	United Forum of Bank Unions
VRS	Voluntary Retirement Scheme
WTO	World Trade Organisation

List of Tables

List of Annexures

1. Exchange of letters between Samar Mukherjee (MP, CPI (M)) and H.M. Patel (Finance Minister 1977-1980) on the issue of implementation of the Pillai Committee Recommendations.
2. Letter written by R.N. Godbole as the convenor of the negotiating committee of the AICOBOO on the issue of wage revision.
3. Some of the resolutions passed in first General Council of the AIBOC.
4. Letter written by the AIBOC to the Chairpersons of all the Regional Rural Banks on the issue of pay parity.
5. Resolutions passed in the second General Council of the AIBOC on the issue of communal harmony and working class unity.
6. Resolutions on the recommendations of the Narasimham Committee passed in the third General Council.
7. Resolution on the New Economic Policies passed by the third General Council of the AIBOC.
8. The UFBU meets the Verma Committee and submits its memorandum on the issue of Weak Public Sector Banks with a special reference to UCO Bank, UBI and the Indian Bank.

Introduction

The problem of looking at white-collar workers as struggling workers has long plagued the theory of class struggle. As we know, the conventional perspective of class struggle is largely about the proletariat who struggle for their existence and rights. But the view that all stages of the labour process experience one or another form of alienation is very much central to Marxist theory. In fact, the level of alienation and subordination in managerial positions was first theorised by Harry Braverman in *Labor and Monopoly Capital: The Degradation of Work in the Twentieth Century* when he spoke about the subordination of the managerial class to capital. The labour regime that Braverman wrote about did not only include manual labour, but also dealt with clerical and managerial labour, showing that the nature of activity was self-alienating as it was directed by the interests of capital.[1] Hence, the managerial classes were in fact alienated knowledge and creative workers whose training and knowledge was not controlled by them. This, itself, was a type of disciplining that did not take the interest of workers into account. In this sense, all managers were workers who were disciplined through the introduction of technology in the office, and uniform labour process across the Industry. As Braverman showed, the mechanisation of the office and the role of accounting procedures in the labour process had created a new class structure within corporations. These new classes could basically be described as clerical and managerial labour that was also used to control the rest of the workers.

Seen in this context, the development of the banking sector is as old as capitalism itself, but the advent of monopoly capitalism has put a new focus on its functioning. As Lenin himself put it, the unity of banking and industrial sectors in terms of the control over capital was characteristic of the development of big monopoly corporations all over the world.[2] As Amiya Kumar Bagchi has shown, the origins of the banking sector lay in the spread of colonial capitalism since the early nineteenth century.[3] By the 1930s, the State Bank of India had grown into a nationwide bank with a large workforce. Its spread, however, was rapid after the process of nationalisation and the merging of all regional banks with the State Bank of India after 1959. The next milestone was the nationalisation of banks, which brought all state owned, and public sector banks under a common umbrella. Common policies that governed these banks also helped to consolidate funds for industrial and priority sector banking. While, nationalisation in itself was a welcome step, it was also accompanied by the development of the Indian bourgeoisie and big business houses. The consolidation of the banking sector had helped the industry to access credit at low interest rates without adequate regulation and disciplining. Thus, it can be safely surmised that the Indian bourgeoisie benefited more than the working classes with the nationalisation of banks, even though there was a considerable improvement in the access to credit of farmers and others.

Though the banks were meant to form the basis of the Indian developmental project, state capitalism ensured that there was no parity in the service conditions of the bank employees. Hence, the need for the organisation of bank employees was felt even before independence. After the formation of the All India Trade Union Congress (AITUC), the first employee union of the Bank employees was formed under the name of All India Bank Employees' Association (AIBEA) in the decade of the 1920s. However, this association represented largely the clerical staff who were the first to organise themselves in the sector. The consciousness of being part of the 'working people' was not ingrained in the officers of the Bank. It was thus necessary to have a continuous process of struggle to develop a strong officers' movement. It is also significant that the officers learnt from other working class movements and were guided by the experience of the clerical staff in the initial years of their organisation.

This book describes the process of organisation of bank officers who represent a large part of the white-collar workers in India. It shows how a class of professional bankers, not only fought for their rights to work with dignity, but also showed sensitivity towards supporting other working class organisations. This process of politicisation was led by the formation of a loose federation at the core of which was the All India Bank Officers' Confederation, which was formed after the realisation that unity amongst all workers in banks was essential to succeed. In this sense the organisation of officers, which started with inspiration from clerical workers was also a catalyst in taking up many working class issues.

This merger helped the bank officers to realise that they were paid differential salaries and had different conditions of work for the same jobs. This was against the principle of equality, which was the foundation of the independent Indian Constitution. In the light of this the formation All India State Bank Officers' Federation highlighted the need for parity and begun to campaign for it amongst different employees and officers of different banks. The result of this vigorous campaigning and politicisation was the famous 1969 strike, which was a defining moment in the struggle of the officers. Led by pioneers of the movement, L.V. Subramaniam and A.V. Rajwade, the strike showed that bank officers were not part of the management and that their alienation from their own capabilities was structured by technical and other developments in the economy, which had a bearing on the banking sector as a whole. The process of formalization of a Confederation began after the strike and culminated in the formation of the All India Confederation of Bank Officers' Organisations (AICOBOO). The AIBOC came into existence in 1985 due to difference of opinion among the leaders of the AICOBOO. This book illustrates, in great detail, the making of the AIBOC and its activities as it expanded and developed its scope.

It shows that the officers were bothered, not only about their working conditions but also about the future of the economy as a whole. In the last few decades, this factor has structured the character of the struggles and made the bank officers an important part of the fight against neo-liberalism. The core values of bank officers were derived from larger democratic and progressive politics which touched every section of the post-independent society in India. One prominent recent example of this is the fact that the AIBOC opposed rules regarding the minimum balance accounts because this would be against the principle of financial inclusion since public sector banks were meant to serve ordinary farmers and workers with small holdings. Hence, any infirmities in the working of small accounts should be sorted out by a democratic and accountable system and not merely by shutting down all small accounts. Another important political struggle that has been taken up by the AIBOC is against the privatization of the banking sector. Like other trade unions, the AIBOC too believes that reforms like the Financial Resolution and Deposit Insurance Bill introduced in the Indian Parliament will go against the interests of the depositors and lead to the dissolution of banking institutions, thus opening up financial markets and putting at risk the savings of many salaried and working people. By spearheading the political campaign against privatization of the banking sector, the AIBOC placed itself in a leadership position within the larger fight against financial and labour law reforms. The inter-linkages between the two are illustrated through the AIBOC campaign; financial reforms would lead to the domination of private capital in the banking sector and also lead to the contractualisation of jobs and the reduction in the benefits of bank officers themselves.

An important aspect of the AIBOC's work has been the creative strategies that it has used to organise the managerial class not only for agitations, but also for other types of activities that promoted workers welfare. Thus, the constituents of the AIBOC run schools and support livelihood activities for different sections of society. They also partner with universities and other academic institutions to undertake research on subjects that are relevant to their own struggles. In this way, the bank officers connect with other movements with similar goals of democratizing society.

This book recounts the history of the All India Bank Officers' Confederation and illustrates some of the propositions made above. Rather, than being an exhaustive account of events, it provides some glimpses of the important moments in the struggle of this managerial class. In doing so, it strengthens the argument that changes within the structure of capitalism have continuously transformed the complex nature of the working class. Thus, there is a greater need to focus on documenting the collective actions of different types of organisations. This is largely because the historiography of working class movements has largely taken cognizance of the movements of factory workers at the lower end of surplus extraction. However, the different layers and institutional forms through which surplus is extracted from different sections of the working class remains understudied in current scholarship. This documentation of the struggles of the bank officers fills this gap to a certain extent and adds the available literature on the history of the banking sector.

The book is divided into four chapters apart from the introduction and conclusion. The first chapter provides an overview of the early struggles and forms of organisation of the bank employees. The second chapter recounts the processes that led to the birth of the AIBOC and discusses the evolution of the democratic decision making process in the organisation. The third chapter provide details and accounts of different negotiations and agreements that have been a part of the struggle of the AIBOC. The fourth chapter of the book outlines milestones in the history of the AIBOC and some of the current struggles and challenges before the organisation. This book is largely based on the documents of the organisation, writings of some of its seminal leaders and interviews with retired bank officers who were once the leaders of the Confederation. The book is dedicated to the memory and work of all those who led by example and showed how a militant organisation can be built through struggles of workers in managerial and supervisory roles. It also highlights the struggles for larger national cause, which the AIBOC has lead in various forms and also with UFBU.

Notes

1. Harry Braverman, *Labor and Monopoly Capital; The Degradation of Work in the Twentieth Century* (New York: Monthly Review Press, 1974).
2. V.I. Lenin, *Imperialism: The Highest Stage of Capitalism* (1917) (Leftword Books, 2000 Reprint).
3. Amiya Kumar Bagchi, *The Evolution of the State Bank of India* (Bombay: Oxford University Press, 1987).

1
Early Working Class Movement in the Banking Sector
Laying the Foundation for the AIBOC

The All India Bank Officers' Confederation (AIBOC) traces its history in the first countrywide Confederation of Bank Officers' Organisations, called the All India Confederation of Bank Officers' Organisations (AICOBOO), which was formed in 1969. The Officers started organising themselves in a systematic way by the end of the 1960s and were very much influenced by the employees' trade unions. The trade unionism among bank employees dates back to the colonial era. It was an integral part of the larger Indian Trade Union Movement, which grew alongside India's struggle for independence and played an important role in liberating the country from colonial rule[1]. The question that arises is how, why and in what conditions did the working class in the Indian banking sector organised itself and became an important component of these larger struggles. This chapter seeks to answer this question by tracing the evolution of trade unionism among bank employees and their role in laying the foundations for the officer's union.

The Evolution of the Indian Banking Sector

The modern system of banking in India has its roots in the colonial period and evolved because of changes in trade and relations of the Indian economy with the economy of Europe. Initially, English agency houses began to serve as bankers to the

East India Company. The agency houses accepted deposits, lent money to merchants, ship-owners, ship managers, governments and generally helped finance external trade.[2] The first of these was the Hindustan Bank, which was established in 1770 by the agency house of Alexander and Company in Kolkata. There were many chartered banks established by different agency houses from different European countries.

However, it was only from the year 1773, when the Regulation Act was passed by the British Parliament, which led to the subordination of the East India Company's government in India to the British Parliament. To protect its financial interest in India, banks were established under the acts of colonial government's legislature, which were divided into two groups.[3] The first consisted of three presidency banks, which included Bank of Bengal established in 1806 as Bank of Calcutta, Bank of Bombay and Bank of Madras established in 1840 and 1843 respectively. They were given this nomenclature because the operations of East India Company were also divided into the three presidencies. These banks were later amalgamated into the Imperial Bank of India in 1920. The other group consisted of the Indian joint-stock banks. The joint-stock banks started in large numbers in India, especially after the passing of the Charter Act in 1813, which permitted Europeans settling in India to establish banks with unlimited liabilities. Encouraged by this, several banks were established mainly by the English and European agency houses. However, half of them failed by 1860. Therefore, the Act VII was passed in 1860 permitting the starting of a joint-stock based on limited liabilities. The point to note here is that, all these banks were managed by mostly Europeans and no Indian owned the bank until the establishment of Oudh Commercial Bank in 1881. It was followed by the 'Punjab National Bank' and the 'People's Bank of India' established in 1894 and 1901 respectively.

When the Imperial Bank of India was established in 1920, the intention was to develop it into a full-fledged central bank. However, when the Hilton Young Currency Commission was appointed in 1926, it recommended that a separate central bank called the Reserve Bank of India should be established for the same purpose. The commission also recommended that the central bank should be free from all political influence; therefore, it should not have any government representative on its Board of Directors. However, the British Government did not agree to this and therefore changes were made to the recommendations of the Hilton Young Currency Commission. This resulted in the establishment of the Reserve Bank of India in 1935 through an Act of the British Parliament. However, in both the Imperial Bank as well as the Reserve Bank of India, the supervising staff remained largely non-Indian until 1930.[4] In all the banks, whether under the imperial government or owned by Indians, the employees had a very difficult time as their working day could extend till almost midnight. In one instance where a sub-staff member in the Bank of India was severely ill because of his asthmatic conditions, but he was not granted leave. Upon taking a leave by himself for three days, he was dismissed from service.[5]

Emergence of Working Class Organisation in the Banking Sector

These stories were common amongst most commercial banks in spite of bank-level struggles in different parts of India against such inhume conditions. Bombay and Calcutta were the centres of these struggles. In Bombay, the Bank of India employees took a lead in initiating this struggle. They formed a union on 16 March 1946 and within a few months, went on 13-day strike on 23 July 1946. This forced the management into a negotiation with the union and finally, a negotiated bipartite settlement was reached in a commercial bank for the first time. This settlement was also gazetted by the Bombay Government as a consent award given by Divatia Tribunal[6] on 15 September 1946. The award given by Divatia Tribunal was made applicable to 4,500 employees henceforth referred to as 'award staffs'. The tribunal divided banks in two groups: big banks and small banks. Based on this division, salaries were fixed to clerks, peons and sweepers. The salary for the clerical staff in big banks ranged from Rs. 65 to Rs. 275, whereas in small banks it was between Rs. 55 and Rs. 250. It also included a provision for dearness allowance and certain leave rules. This gave a ray of hope to the employees in other banks and all the bank employees in and around Bombay formed unions and came together to form Bombay Bank Employees Federation. The Federation submitted a charter of demands to thirty banks and since there was no response from the management, they went on a strike for 11 days. The Government of Bombay was forced to intervene and all the disputes in different banks were referred to an Industrial Tribunal under the chairpersonship of Justice Divatia.[7]

These were times when India was fighting against the British rule and this movement saw participation by all sections of society. Peasants and workers had a major role to play in making this movement a mass movement. The trade union movement was also picking up in the country with the formation of the All India Trade Union Congress (AITUC) in 1920. All struggles of the workers of this country were brought under one central trade union organisation and it was a major part of the fight against British rule. In 1946, the struggling bank employees were also organised under the umbrella of one central federation, which was named the All India Bank Employees' Association (AIBEA). Even though there were bank level unions, they were not recognised as trade unions by the British Government. The first registered union to be formed in the banking sector was the Imperial Bank of India Indian Staff Association on 9 July 1920, which was registered under the Benevolent Societies Act.[8] There were similar unions in Allahabad Bank and Bank of India, but these unions had no bargaining power and could only write applications and appeal to the management to look into the grievances of workers. This situation ended with the formation of the AIBEA, to whom most of the bank employees' organisations sought affiliation. Employees now started asserting their right to a dignified working environment and they started organising into trade unions. They gave strike calls, held protest demonstrations and used other methods of collective bargaining.

Although an All India organisation had been formed and solidarity actions were undertaken, struggles were largely confined to the state level. A major initiative in shaping the trade union movement was undertaken by the then Bengal Circle of the Imperial Bank of India Indian Staff Association, which gave the first ever indefinite strike call in the banking sector on 1 August 1946 in Bengal, Orissa, Bihar and the North East. This strike lasted for 46 days and many demands like a 40 per cent increase in the salary, introduction of leave rules, free medical aid and medical reimbursement for family, gratuity for non-pensionable staff were put forth by the association. Finally, upon interventions from leading political leaders like Jawaharlal Nehru and Jayaprakash Narayan,[9] the unions secured an interim relief of 25 per cent increase in the salary for the employees and a tribunal was set by the Bengal Government under the chairpersonship of R. Gupta, which gave its award on 12 May 1947. Similar struggles were taken up in different parts of the country, which led to the formation of different state-level and bank level awards like the B.B. Singh Award for Uttar Pradesh, S.C. Chakraborty Award and S. Sen Award for the employees of Imperial Bank of India and Central Bank respectively. Because the disputes in banking industry were resolved through state-level tribunals and awards, the period between 1946 and 1949 is known as the era of state-level tribunals.[10]

With the independence of India, it was natural for the workers to expect better wages and better working conditions from the newly elected government. There were a number of regulations brought in to protect the interest of the workers like the Factories Act, Industrial Dispute Act and Minimum Wage Act, etc. In consideration of the difficulties faced in implementing state-level awards in banks, having branches in more than one state, the central government assumed powers of jurisdiction for settlement of industrial dispute in the banking industry. After taking over the jurisdiction, the government appointed a three-member national tribunal with Justice K.C. Sen as chairperson on 13 June 1949.[11] All 170 banks (including 82 scheduled banks and 88 non-scheduled banks)[12] were part of their terms of reference and 64 unions including 13 regional unions and 51 bank wise unions participated in the proceedings of the Sen Tribunal. The Sen Award categorised banks based on their average working funds into three groups of 'A' class banks with working fund of Rs. 25 Crores and above, 'B' class banks included banks with working fund between Rs. 7.5 Crores to Rs. 25 Crores and 'C' class banks with less than Rs. 7.5 Crores working fund. Each class of banks were further divided into different areas based on their area of functioning. Banks in the metro-cities of Ahmedabad, Bombay, Calcutta and Delhi were grouped into Area I. Towns with a population between fifty thousand and one lakh were grouped together as area II. All other places were grouped as Area III. Based on these groupings, a pay scale was fixed for each groups with a maximum pay of Rs. 290 for employees of Area I of class 'A' banks and a minimum of Rs. 191 for the employees of Area III of class 'C' banks. The recommendations of the Sen Tribunal were considered to be very progressive by the bank employees as uniform service conditions were recommended for the first time at an all India level. The award suggested fixed working hours, specific pay structure, Dearness Allowance (D.A), House Rent Allowance (H.R.A) (though only for five centres), uniforms and washing allowances, bonus, and gratuity along with other benefits. It also suggested that the union representatives should be entitled to Duty Leave, Travel Allowance (T.A) and Halting Allowance for attending the Industrial Tribunal. The tribunal also recommended for amendment of Provision 33 of the Industrial Dispute Act in order to prevent unilateral punitive measures by the management including termination from services due to the absence of leaders for attending the tribunals. Bank employees were unhappy with the classification of banks on the basis of place of operation but by and large they were happy with the recommendations of Sen Award. However, management of banks were unhappy with the award as it reduced their power and therefore, they filed a court case against the Sen Tribunal. The Supreme Court declared the award void on the grounds that one of the members of the tribunal (i.e., Justice N. Chandrasekhar Iyer) was absent from the hearing.[13]

Thereafter, the Government of India brought the banking industry within the purview of the industrial disputes with the enactment of the Industrial Disputes (Banking and Insurance Companies) Act, of 1949, which was passed on 14 December 1949.[14] From then onwards, the industrial disputes in the banking sector were resolved by national level tribunals. Between 1949 and 1966, many national tribunals were set up which gave their respective awards, which were applicable to bank employees. The Sastry Tribunal was the first in this series, which gave its award on 26 March 1953. The award was made applicable from 1 April 1953. In the Sastry Award, the division based on place of work remained same as the Sen Award, but it included another class, i.e., 'D' class, banks. This class included banks with a working fund of less than Rs. 1 Crore. The proposed pay scale for each group was lower in this award in comparison with the proposal of the Sen Award, especially in the case of the newly created 'D' class and therefore employees were unhappy with this award.

A new phase in banking history began when the Imperial Bank of India was taken over by the Government of India on 1 July 1955 and the State Bank of India (SBI) was constituted with the enactment of the State Bank of India Act, 1955. With a change in name and the functioning of the bank, the union also changed its name and style of functioning. In the same year, the union changed its name to All India State Bank of India Staff Federation (AISBISF). Its main objective was to ensure that the Shastry Award was made uniformly applicable to all employees, since many new employees had been recruited as part of the expansion of SBI. The 'D' group employees in SBI were paid a meagre amount, which was much less than the one recommended by the Sastry Award.[15] However, the government informed the union that it could not afford to pay all employees the same salary and this led to a sense of dissatisfaction which finally culminated in the strike of 1960, which went on for 21 days starting from the 4 March 1955.

Finally, at the end of the strike, the K.T. Desai tribunal was appointed which released its award on 13 June 1962 and covered 80,000 employees working in 84 banks. Desai Award again shifted to the categorisation of banks into three groups with a maximum pay of Rs. 405. The Award also gave a full neutralisation in dearness allowance to the members of 'subordinate' staff. It also gave provision of a few other allowances along with provident fund, pension and gratuity. Though the award fell below the expectation of the employees, still it was an improvement in comparison to previous awards. All these years of national-level tribunals, popularly known as the era of national tribunals, there was an improvement in pay scales, working conditions and emoluments, at the same time, trade unionism grew among bank employees in terms of both membership as well as activities. It is because of all these awards, which used to govern the working conditions and pay structure of the clerks and subordinate staffs, they are popularly known as award staff and their unions as award staff unions.

At this time, the AIBEA was leading the bank employees' struggle. The two demands that were constantly raised by AIBEA throughout its 11th, 12th and 13th conferences were regarding the nationalisation of the banking industry and the industry level direct negotiations between bankers and employees for the settlement of demands. The term of the Desai Award was to expire on the 31 December 1962, before which the government gave it an extension of a year till 31 December 1963. The employees under the leadership of AIBEA submitted a charter of demands asking a wage increase of 20 per cent. However, this demand was neglected and Desai Award was yet again extended till 31 December 1964. Since the demands of employees were neglected, AIBEA started a non-cooperation movement throughout the country from 20 July 1964 to demand a bipartite settlement. Under the impact of the movement, the entire banking operation in the country came to a standstill and its pressure was felt by both the government and the bankers. Through the intervention of the Chief Labour Commissioner (Central), a tripartite meeting was held between the AIBEA and the IBA (Indian Banks' Association) and EBA (Exchange Banks' Association). In the tripartite meeting, a memorandum of settlement was signed on 18 August 1964, where the management was forced to give an immediate ad-hoc increase of two extra slabs of Dearness Allowance and also to start industry-level negotiations for settlement of the workers demand.[16]

Similarly, the State Bank of India Staff Federation also demanded a bipartite negotiation with the bank's management as the tribunals took a long time to dispense their awards and above that, it was often observed that the management and the government would refuse the implementation of all recommendations of the awards. Finally, they also had their first bipartite agreement with the management on 19 October 1966. Thus, the era of tribunals ended in the banking industry and the process of bipartite settlements began thereafter.[17] This was in fact the first step towards the further organisation of the bank officers. This process is discussed in the subsequent sections.

The Era of Bipartite Negotiations

With the institutionalisation of the bipartite, staff unions were getting stronger, through successive bipartite negotiations, they were able to secure better working conditions and a better pay. All these achievements were gained even while officers were neglected by both the management and the government. The employees' trade unions catered mainly to the interests of the clerical and 'subordinate staff' and considered 'officers' as part of the management. Therefore, the relations between the two groups were not cordial. However, from the very beginning when officers had started organising themselves, they insisted on forming organisations based upon the model of the employees' unions. This poses a question regarding reasons for officers to organise themselves as trade unions. Another question that is posed is regarding the differences between employees' organisations and officers' organisations.

Earlier the bank officers considered themselves as a part of the management, though they hardly had any say in the decision-making. However, the expanding banking sector with the increasing number of supervising staff and head cashiers enhanced the distance between the decision maker and those who had to implement it. Thus, the myth of officers being part of management was shattered. Officers could also see that the award staff through their trade unionism had been able to secure better pay scales, working conditions and other allowances.[18] The achievements secured by the award staff unions through tribunals and subsequent bipartite settlement had put the officers in a relatively worse position as the award staff received a comparatively larger in-hand salary than officers did. The working conditions were harsh, as officers had to work longer hours; even leave was at the mercy of management. Further, and social security measures like provident fund, medical facilities and gratuity were unavailable to officers.[19]

The AICOBOO and the Formation of the Officers' Movement

During this time, many officers were promoted from award staff to supervisor positions. One such person was L.V. Subramaniam, who was in the forefront of organising officers in the city of Bombay. He joined the banking industry in 1952 as a clerk in a small town of Madhya Pradesh called Jabalpur. He was part of a staff union organisation when he was in Jabalpur and had a major contribution in organising the bank employees of Madhya Pradesh during the 1960s strike. He joined as an officer in the year 1964, which was when he was transferred to Bombay. For the next two years, he contemplated reverting to clerk post because of the better salary and working conditions. Since the State Bank of India was expanding its reach to the remote regions of the country, there were many like him who joined after a promotion and had seen Subramaniam as a leader of award staff. They showed faith in his leadership and told him to organise the supervising staff to improve their working conditions.[20] A majority of the people who were at the forefront of the trade union movement were officers, who had been promoted from award staff. Those who joined directly as officers were also dissatisfied with the working conditions, but their cultural and social notions were pushing them from trade union activities as trade unions were considered as the organisation of blue-collar employees. However, the directly recruited officers were also an important part of the movement, though in less numbers. Directly recruited officers like P. G. Kakodkar and A.V. Rajwade were leading the movement. A.V. Rajwade was the President of the SBI Officers' Federation during the indefinite strike 1969 and gave a direction to the movement. However, since the award staff unions were quite successful in organising the bank employees and articulating their demands, this inspired the officers' leaders to organise themselves on the lines of award staff unions. There were a few, who were reluctant to form a trade union. However, the reluctant members agreed after some persuasion and the Bombay circle of the SBI formed its association in January 1965.[21] Similar efforts were made in the other states by the State Bank officers; Bengal was the first state to have an officers association, which registered itself under the Societies Registration Act in the year 1962.[22] By 1965, many circle level associations had already been formed. The leaders also realised that since the decision-making had been centralised, the officers should also form an all India federation to negotiate with the management. Thus, on 29 and 30 August 1965 representatives of the Bengal, Ahmedabad, Bombay, Delhi, Hyderabad, Kanpur and Madras circle came together in Bombay to form the All India State Bank of India Supervising Staff Federation (AISBISSF). L.V. Subramaniam was elected as the General Secretary and S.K. Mishra as President of the new organisation. It was this organisation, which shaped the destiny of bank officers' movement.

The year 1969 is extremely important for the banking sector in India, as 14 banks were nationalised. This year is also important for the workers' movement in the banking sector as the officers of State Bank of India under the leadership of AISBISSF went on an indefinite strike. This was the first indefinite strike call by a 'white collar' trade union. This indefinite strike was the culmination of all the injustices that the officers had to face in their workplace, which lasted for 17 days.[23] At the end of the strike, the State Bank management recognised the existence of an officers' organisation and started negotiations with them, though it was still not formally recognised as a trade union by the Indian State. Such a show of strength by the State Bank officers gave the officers across banks and across the nation a hope that even officers can be a part of trade unions and they too have the right of collective bargaining.

Similar to the State Bank of India the situation of officers in other banks was tragic. Resentment started developing among officers and the same officers, for whom it was earlier unconceivable to be a part of trade unions, started to organise themselves. Thus, by the end of 1960s many bank level federations/associations came into existence in banks like the Bank of India, the Central Bank of India, the State Bank of India, the UCO Bank, the Union Bank, the Dena Bank, the Canara Bank and others.[24] With this motivation gained from the 1969 movement, bank-level unions were making efforts to negotiate wages with their respective managements, but an All India Officers' Organisation had become essential because of the nationalisation of banks in 1969. This need was fulfilled by the formation of the All India Confederation of Bank Officers' Organisation (AICOBOO) with L.V. Subramaniam as General Secretary and A.R. Sule of the Bank of India as the Chairperson.[25] the AICOBOO started functioning by 1969, however, it was formally recognised by the Government of India only in 1971. From the very beginning, efforts were made by the leadership of the AICOBOO to take the problems of bank officers from the bank level to the national level as the salary structure for officers was arbitrarily fixed by the individual bank's management. Many issues like salaries, the merger of grades, promotion policy, issues regarding dearness allowance and house rent allowance, working hours, disciplinary procedures, housing loan, transfer policy, etc. confronted the AICOBOO. Its first task was to press for the standardisation of working conditions amongst the officers of different banks. At the time of its formation, there were many discrepancies in the salaries, fitment formula and working conditions between officers of different banks. To solve this problem, a committee called the 'Committee for Standardisation of Pay Scales, Allowances and Perquisites of Officers in the Nationalised Banks' was appointed in the year 1973 with Professor U.R. Pillai as Chairperson, on whose name the committee is popularly known as the Pillai Committee.[26] The committee submitted its report to the government in a record time of ten months on 30 May 1974.[27] The officers' unions and the AICOBOO deposed before the committee and submitted their charter of demands.[28] The Pillai Committee recommended a standardised pay scale and other service conditions for officers in all the nationalised banks. However, during the same time, the emergency was declared by the Indian government and all the activities of trade unions were restricted. Even in the banking sector, a service conduct rule was imposed on bank employees and officers; thus, forbidding them from participating in any trade union activities.[29] In addition, the discussions and implantation of the Pillai Committee Recommendations (PCR) was postponed indefinitely.

The banking industry was excluded from the Bonus Act in the same period and this created frustration and resentment amongst bank workers. The worst part of this was that bank employees were told to refund the bonus already paid for 1974 and the interim bonus paid for the half of 1975.[30] The unprecedented price rise accompanied with budget cut through such measures made situation the worse for the officers. The resentment was conveyed to the government with the initiation of protest action. However, there were hardly any steps taken by the government in that direction; instead, all the facilities enjoyed by the officers' associations and federations were taken away.

The situation started to change only after the change in government in 1977 when the new government under the Prime Ministership of Morarji Desai came to power. The hostility and fear disappeared and there arose great expectations among the officers' organisations.[31] The first hope that came to the officers was when the banking industry was brought under the purview of the Bonus Act. Another important development was the incorporation of members belonging to majority unions being inducted into the boards of banks. It was also hoped that the long-standing demand of the officers' organisation to widen the definition of 'workmen' in the Industrial Dispute Act to bring them under the protection of this rule would finally be fulfilled as the new government had shown interest in rationalising and updating the Act. However, the joy of this partial victory was short lived because an amendment was made in Section 34 of the Bonus Act, which mandated that bonus be related to the disclosed profits of the banks and the balance sheets of banks did not disclose the correct profits made by the institutions. Similarly, the Industrial Dispute Bill, which was introduced in the parliament not only excluded the officers' organisations but also precluded them from registering their unions.

For any government to make changes in the banking industry, the problem of anomalies needed to be resolved first. Therefore, the new government once again appointed a study group of bankers to make suggestions for the implementation of the Pillai Committee Report. The study group modified certain recommendations and submitted its report. This study group of bankers mainly consisted of bank management; therefore, the officers' unions opposed the unilateral implementation of the Pillai Committee. They wanted that their opinion should also be incorporated in the changes made to the Pillai Committee Recommendations; therefore, they demanded the implementation of PCR only through the bipartite negotiations.

On 27 September 1977, the AICOBOO went on a one-day strike to protest against the management and the government's neglect and indifference to hear the officers' problems. The following demands were put forth: 1) Removal of draconian conduct rules imposed on officers during the emergency. 2) Standardisation of service conditions of bank officers only through bipartite negotiations. 3) Reinstatement of bank officers wrongfully retired/terminated and victimised during the emergency. 4) Restoration of rights to negotiate bonus. 5) Restoration of trade union rights of collective bargaining. 6) Statutory protection for bank officers. This protest also received support from employees unions in banking industry and unions in other financial institutions like Life Insurance Corporation (LIC) and Reserve Bank of India (RBI). The situation of bank officers also got the attention of political parties and leaders particularly of the left organisations. Discussing the right of officers' organisation to negotiate their wages, many letters were exchanged between Samar Mukherjee, who was an M.P. from Communist Party of India (Marxist) to H.M Patel, the then Union Finance Minister (Annexure 1). The letter written by Samar Mukherjee explains the importance of bipartite negotiations when it says: 'the bank officers are more concerned about their hard earned trade union rights which were intended to be taken away by the Government of India by imposing unilaterally the said terms and conditions in the name of standardisation.'

The success of the above-mentioned protest was felt all across the country and finally, the AICOBOO got a letter from the Indian Banks' Association (IBA) for making a submission of their opinion on the Pillai Committee Report. This would form the basis for further discussions, which were held in two rounds in February and March 1979. There were multiple protests called by the AICOBOO on the issue of the unilateral implementation of the Pillai Committee. However, the dialogue could not reach any conclusion and the PCR were implemented on 1 January 1979. However, it was decided that the implementation would be only done through bank level negotiations with the recognised officers' associations.[32] The two major points of dispute were the categorisation of posts and the national dearness allowance. Although the struggles by bank level federations, managements of most of the banks came for negotiations and bank level bipartite settlements could be reached. Thus, the PCR were passed by the boards of all the 14 nationalised banks in June 1979. In this manner, the revised terms of the PCR became effective in these banks from 1 July 1979. In August 1977, the government announced that the PCR would also be applicable to the State Bank of India, which was not a part of terms of reference of the Pillai Committee. Thus, the State Bank officers formally signed an agreement on 23 November 1979 after intense negotiations. The Central Board of Directors of the bank at its meeting at Ahmedabad on 19 December 1979 passed the necessary order to give effect to the agreement on the revised PCR and thus it was implemented and was made applicable to the State Bank of India (SBI), its subsidiaries with some modifications and 14 nationalised banks as it is. The final PCR divided the officers into four standardised grades given in table 1, based on identification of broad level responsibility and each grade had one or more scale.[33]

Table 1: Pay Scales and Grades of Officers in accordance with PCR

Grade	*Scales*	
Top Executive	VI	VII
Senior Management	IV	V
Middle Management	II	III
Junior Management	I	

The standardisation of pay scales and service conditions brought about through the implementation of the PCR made it imperative for the officers' organisations to have negotiations at the industry level. However, mere standardisation was not enough and a revision of pay scales was required to solve the outstanding problems and discrepancies that remained because of the award staff having completed their third bipartite settlement. The starting pay for officers was Rs. 700 per month when the PCR was implemented and at that time the maximum pay for clerical scale was Rs. 550, but after the third bipartite for award staff, the clerical scale went up to Rs. 1,040 per month, whereas the officers' pay did not have any revision. The Reserve Bank of India had also evolved a pay structure starting at Rs. 900 per month. Therefore, a charter of demands was submitted to the Indian Banks' Association (IBA) by the AICOBOO on 18 June 1980[34] demanded parity in pay scale with the employees of RBI. Consistent efforts were made by the AICOBOO to begin talks on the charter of demands as soon as possible and in the same direction, a strike call was planned on the 12 December 1980.[35] However, before the strike could take place an understanding was reached at the level of the Union Finance Minister and the talks with the IBA began. While the talks were still undergoing it came to the notice of the AICOBOO that a committee headed by V.R. Gupta had been appointed to fix pay scales and it had suggested a lower pay scale to the six banks.[36] The idea of different and inferior pay scales based on the date of nationalisation of banks was rejected by the AICOBOO. Thus, in May 1981, the AICOBOO submitted a revised charter of demands, which included issues like dearness allowance, increment, increase in the ceiling of vehicular loans and other payment-related issues to the standardisation of terms and conditions of service of officers in the six banks nationalised in April 1980. It was finally decided by the government to extend the recommendations of Pillai Committee to the six nationalised banks, which was made effective from 1982.

The First Bipartite Settlement of the Bank Officers and the Formation of the All Bank Officers' Confederation (AIBOC)

By 1982 the PCR were made applicable to SBI, its subsidiaries, (14 nationalised banks and 6 other banks), which were nationalised later. With this, the AICOBOO revised its charter of demands in April 1982, and instructed its members to start a campaign to popularise its charter of demands, as there was a possibility for launching an agitation to pressurise the IBA to start bipartite negotiations with the AICOBOO.[37] Since the bipartite agreement with the employees' unions was to end in August 1982, the IBA started talks with both the award staff organisations and the AICOBOO. During this period, a vast majority of the officers wanted the salary revision of officers to be simultaneous with award staff. The talks between the IBA and the award staff unions began at the same time when the officers' unions started their talks with the IBA. The agreement between the staff unions and the IBA was reached by early June of 1984. Thus, the employees' unions were able to reach a settlement on 17 September 1984 as the government approved that proposal and the settlement came into force retrospectively from the 1 July 1983. The discussion between the IBA and the officers' organisations ended in the end of December 1984 and a settlement was reached. It was expected that like the award staffs' settlements, the officers' settlement too would be approved by the government soon.[38] However, there was an unexpected delay by the government in clearing the settlement. By May 1985, the anxiety had started to build up to such an extent that there were rumours that the AICOBOO had failed to settle the issue of salary revision.[39] There were pressures on the AICOBOO from the affiliate members and a conference of the representatives of the affiliates of the AICOBOO was called on 25 and 26 of May at Hyderabad where the affiliates expressed their dissatisfaction with the leadership. Since there was no decision on the part of the government, which neither accepted nor rejected the settlement, it was decided that there was no need to go into a direct action, but that a delegation of the AICOBOO should meet the Finance Minister to convey the anxieties of its members. To keep itself ready for any situation, the AICOBOO had also reconstituted the negotiating committee and set-up an enlarged action committee.[40] R.N. Godbole, who at that time was the General Secretary of All India Stata Bank Officers' Federation, became the convenor of the negotiating committee.

On 24 June 1985, the negotiating committee of the AICOBOO was informed of the government's clearance of the salary proposals for officers. Immediately, it was decided that the action committee would meet on 25 and 26 June to develop a reaction to the proposal. In this meeting, which was held at Bombay, the General Secretary of the AICOBOO was not present, thus the resentment towards the leadership of the organisation developed even further. With 11 out of 16 present in that meeting, it was decided that a detailed letter would be sent to the IBA conveying the reaction of the committee. It was further decided that all affiliates should hold their Executive Committee (E.C.) meeting to formulate their viewpoint on the final stand to be taken by the AICOBOO by 8 July.

On the 27 of June 1985, a detailed letter was written by R.N. Godbole as the convenor of the negotiating committee of the AICOBOO to the Chairperson of the IBA pointing out the dissatisfaction with the government's sweeping changes made to the proposal made by the mutual consultation of officers, their organisations and the IBA. There were disagreements on many issues like cost of revision, the pattern of neutralisation, incremental pattern, the merger of dearness allowances and the date of effect (Annexure 2). Instead of listening to those grievances put forth by the officers, the IBA replied that they did not think that any sweeping changes had been made to the agreed proposal.

The negotiating committee accused the AICOBOO of the lack of leadership and pointed out that it had stopped even collecting its subscription fee from its affiliates. It was said that the AICOBOO was largely relying on foreign funds for its functioning and therefore had neglected their own trade union functions. However, L.V. Subramaniam, who was the General Secretary of the AICOBOO, refuted all those allegations.[41] As the officers' wage negotiation was getting delayed, there were many officers who were dissatisfied with the leadership, so they met at Hyderabad on 8 July 1985. The leaders who assembled included S. Roy Chowdhury, Sunil Mukherjee, M.U. Pai, K.S. Shetty, A.K. Jana, K.N. Kannan, the Circle General Secretaries of State Bank Officers' Federation, M. Kantharia, M.L. Gala, S.S. Debholkar, T.S.K. Chari and many others.[42] The organisations represented were from the Bank of India, the State Bank of India, the UCO Bank, the UBI, the Syndicate Bank, the Indian Bank and the Laxmi Vilas Bank. Thus, from then onwards there was a division into the bank officers' movement with the rebel group still functioning within the AICOBOO. The rebel group set-up a committee for the follow-up action at the government level. It was decided that this action plan would take place in the August of 1985. The action plan included a demonstration at the state and district headquarters and other centres where there were a sufficient number of officers. This action materialized into reality on 10 and 12 August 1985 and culminated in a total strike on 13 August 1985.[43] Since the rebel group constituted the majority of the AICOBOO, they were successfully able to persuade the General Secretary to take up the action plan. The successful implementation of the strike gave an enthusiasm to the members but the fight amongst the leaders continued. After the intervention by H.R. Shenoy, H. Ranghavendra and R.C. Agarwal (General Secretaries of the Syndicate Bank Officers' Association, SBI Associate Banks' Officers' Association and All India Central Bank Officers' Federation respectively) and S. Seetharaman (President of the AICBOF), it was agreed that a united front should be presented by the officers till the ensuing triennial conference.[44] While the wage revision was going on, the disagreement between the two groups reached its culmination point at the third triennial conference of the AICOBOO, which was held on 19 of August 1985 at Madras. Those officers' organisations and their leaders who did not participate or walked out in the triennial conference, decided to meet at Delhi on 4 September 1985. In that meeting, it was finally decided to form a new central organisation of officers. However, before that the immediate task taken up by the rebel group was to finalise the wage negotiation. For this reason, they claimed the right to negotiate with the IBA.

Since they had a majority of officers with them, out of 1,75,000 bank officers at that point in time, this group had 1,22,000 officers.[45] IBA was also forced to recognise the group and above that, the group took majority status from the AICOBOO. The negotiation of this group started with the IBA under the name "Group of certain officers' associations." The agreement was finally reached and the settlement was signed on the 24 September 1985, which was implemented retrospectively from the 1 February 1984. Thus, this became the first bipartite settlement for officers, which was the fourth bipartite settlement of the banking industry. Immediately after the salary revision was finalised the group decided to launch the new organisation and thus the All India Bank Officers' Confederation (AIBOC) was formed on 6 October 1985.

Thus, the formation of the AIBOC was preceded by a long history of working class movements in the banking sector. The organisation of award staff first under the colonial rule, then in independent India gave a cue to the officers to organise themselves against harsh working conditions. Majorly the officers promoted from award staff were at the forefront of the early officers' movement. These officers gave a militant shape to the officers' movement and they organised themselves as trade unions. The AICOBOO became the first national level organisation in the banking sector and played a major role in opposing the unilateral imposition of Pillai Committee Report, which became the basis for the subsequent bipartite settlements. However, it was unsuccessful in securing wage revisions on time. This created a resentment among the officers and a group representing the aspirations of the officers for the better pay structure became vocal within the organisation, which later on formed itself into the AIBOC. In the next chapter, we shall look at how the AIBOC formed itself into a democratic organisation and organised the professional workers first in banking sector and then in the financial sector.

Notes

1. Chaman Lal Revri, *The Indian Trade Union Movement: An Outline History 1880-1947* (New Delhi: Orient Longman, 1972), 5.
2. Amiya Kumar Bagchi, *The Evolution of the State Bank of India* (Bombay: Oxford University Press, 1987), 32.
3. S.G. Panandikar, *Banking in India* (Calcutta: Orient Longmans), 5.
4. Ibid., 285.
5. Shanti R. Bal et al., *History of Bank Employees Movement*, ed. Jayanta Roy (West Bengal: Bank Employees Federation of India Publication, 2015), 117.
6. The industrial disputes in the banking industry used to be settled through government appointed tribunals, whose recommendations were called awards.
7. Shanti R. Bal et al., *History of Bank Employees Movement*, ed. Jayanta Roy (West Bengal: Bank Employees Federation of India Publication, 2015), 130.
8. D.T. Franco Rajendra Dev, *Glimpses of the Historic Indefinite Strike 1969* (Bangalore: All India State Bank of India Officers Federation, 2009), 19.

9. Ibid., 20.
10. Shanti R. Bal et al., *History of Bank Employees Movement*, ed. Jayanta Roy (West Bengal: Bank Employees Federation of India Publication, 2015), 137.
11. Ibid., 122.
12. Those banks, which are included in the second schedule of Reserve Bank of India (RBI) Act 1934, are called scheduled banks and these banks have to follow the conditions laid down by the RBI. Whereas those banks which are not included in the schedule are called non-scheduled banks.
13. Shanti R. Bal et al., *History of Bank Employees Movement*, ed. Jayanta Roy (West Bengal: Bank Employees Federation of India Publication, 2015), 148.
14. Usha S. Kanhere, *Managerial Trade Unionism: A Sociological Study of Officers Association in Nationalized Banks in Ahmedabad* (Delhi: Mittal Publications, 1987), 28.
15. L.V. Subramaniam (Former Secretary General of the AICOBOO), interviewed by Sarika Chaudhary, Bangalore, India, February 2018.
16. Shanti R. Bal et al., *History of Bank Employees Movement*, ed. Jayanta Roy (West Bengal: Bank Employees Federation of India Publication, 2015), 202.
17. D.T. Franco Rajendra Dev, *Glimpses of the Historic Indefinite Strike 1969* (Bangalore: All India State Bank of India Officers Federation, 2009), 21.
18. L.V.Subramaniam (Former Secretary General of the AICOBOO), interviewed by Sarika Chaudhary, Bangalore, India, February 2018.
19. S.R. Sengupta, *Bank Officers' Movement; Perspective and Journey* (Kolkata: Foundation for United Trade Union Research & Education (FUTURE), 2010), 2.
20. L.V. Subramaniam (Former Secretary General of the AICOBOO), interviewed by Sarika Chaudhary, Bangalore, India, February 2018.
21. Ibid.
22. D.T. Franco Rajendra Dev, *Glimpses of the Historic Indefinite Strike 1969* (Bangalore: All India State Bank of India Officers Federation, 2009), 24.
23. Ibid., 99
24. S.R. Sengupta, *Bank Officers' Movement; Perspective and Journey* (Kolkata: Foundation for United Trade Union Research & Education (FUTURE), 2010), 4.
25. Ibid., 5.
26. Virenda Kumar, "Committee for Standardization of Pay Scales, Allowances and Perquisites of Officers in the Nationalised Banks, 1973," in *Committees and Commissions in India*, Vol. XI (New Delhi: Concept, 1994), 228.
27. The report is explained in detail in chapter 3.
28. Usha S. Kanhere, *Managerial Trade Unionism: A Sociological Study of Officers Association in Nationalized Banks in Ahmedabad* (Delhi: Mittal Publications, 1987), 39.
29. Ibid.
30. R.N. Godbole, *Report of the General Secretary to the 10th Annual Conference of All India State Bank of India Supervising Staff Federation*, 1975.

31. R.N. Godbole, *Report of the General Secretary to the 11th Annual Conference of All India State Bank of India Officers' Federation,* 1977.
32. R.N. Godbole, *Report of the General Secretary to the 13th Annual Conference of All India State Bank of India Officers' Federation,* 1980.
33. All India Bank Officer' Confederation, *AIBOC – IBA Joint Notes on Wage Revisions* (Bangalore: All India Bank Officers' Confederation, 2010), 24.
34. R.N. Godbole, ed., "AICOBOO Revives Its Charter of Demands," *Common Bond,* June 1982, 4.
35. S.R. Sengupta, *Bank Officers' Movement; Perspective and Journey* (Kolkata: Foundation for United Trade Union Research & Education (FUTURE), 2010), 21.
36. R.N. Godbole, ed., "Standardisation Scheme for Six Banks," *Common Bond,* July 1982, 3.
37. R.N. Godbole, ed., "AICOBOO Revives Its Charter of Demands," *Common Bond,* June 1982, 4.
38. R.N. Godbole, ed., "Salary Revision," *Common Bond,* May 1985, 1.
39. Ibid.
40. R.N. Godbole, ed., "Gearing up the Organisational Machine," *Common Bond,* June 1985, 1.
41. L.V. Subramaniam (Former Secretary General of the AICOBOO), interviewed by Sarika Chaudhary, Bangalore, India, February 2018.
42. S.R. Sengupta, *Bank Officers' Movement; Perspective and Journey* (Kolkata: Foundation for United Trade Union Research & Education (FUTURE), 2010), 25.
43. R.N. Godbole, ed., "Token Strike on 13th August," *Common Bond,* August 1985, 1.
44. S.R. Sengupta, "Emergence of the AIBOC—Logic Was Inexorable," *Common Bond,* December 1985, 4.
45. S.R. Sengupta, *Bank Officers' Movement; Perspective and Journey* (Kolkata: Foundation for United Trade Union Research & Education (FUTURE), 2010), 27.

2

Birth and Expansion of the All India Bank Officers' Confederation

The discussion in the last chapter has provided an overview of the different organisational forms that the struggles of the bank officers waged before the formation of the AIBOC. Before these struggles, the officers not only faced harsh working conditions but also discriminatory practices by the management. These initial struggles were important because they developed a working class consciousness amongst professional workers and prepared them for further intense struggles. Hence, the phase provided a strong foundation for the formation of a national level federation. This is the context of the birth of the All India Bank Officers' Confederation, which has shown the importance of organising educated professional workers. This chapter provides an overview of the organisational structure and functioning of the AIBOC as an example of the democratic organisation of middle class workers.

The Founding Conference and the Organisational Structure of the AIBOC

The formation of the AIBOC is closely related to and reflects the changing nature of banking in India and its decision-making. During the initial stage of the officers' movement, banks were in private hands and branch managers were considered as the employers and ultimate decision makers, and the officers had to negotiate with them. Therefore, the initial stages of the officers' associations were at the branch level. However, the leadership later realised that the bank management did not take decisions at the branch level, but instead at the corporate level and they realised the need for a bank level federation. Therefore, between 1965 and 1969, many bank level organisations were formed to protect the interests of officers against the exploitation of bank managements. After the nationalisation of banks and the standardisation of pay scales, the negotiations happened at the industry level, this resulted in a need for an industry level organisation. Though the AICOBOO was already in existence, the AIBOC started functioning much before its formalisation as a separate organisation. At that time, it was a horizontal organisation with all its constituents or the dissatisfied members of the AICOBOO came together for the sole purpose of the wage negotiations. Immediately after the wage negotiations, they decided to give a formal structure to the organisation and went ahead with the founding conference on 6 October 1985.

The founding conference of the All India Bank Officers' Confederation took place at the Golden Jubilee Auditorium of the Federation of Indian Chambers of Commerce and Industry (FICCI) at New Delhi, where five hundred bank officers participated to give a new direction to the bank officers' movement. R.N. Godbole, who became the first General Secretary of the new organisation, held a firm belief that it was the deficiencies in the constitution of the AICOBOO, which led it to lose its priorities. Therefore, he believed that a well thought-out constitution and well-defined goals were extremely important for the organisation to function well. Drawing upon the experience and in consultation with several other leaders, he along with other members prepared a draft of the constitution, which was approved by all the members of the conference. This constitution became the basis of the organisation of the AIBOC. It provided an outline of the organisational structure, which was based on the federal vertical model of organisation.

A group can organise itself in many ways and the structure of an organisation indicates the relative position of its constituents determining the scope of their respective functions and the degree of mutual dependence in the common endeavour.[1] The organisational structure of a trade union not only determines the strength and cohesion of membership, but also plays an important role in shaping inter-union relations, union policies and the decision making of the union. The organisational structure can be either horizontal or vertical. In a horizontal organisation, the hierarchy of authority is non-existent and units are on the same level with their respective spheres of activity. The constituent members come together to form a council or board, where their representatives discuss matters of common concern. However, in a vertical organisation, the relationship between the constituents is hierarchical and can be either federal or unitary. In a unitary organisation, the central body with direct membership of the constituents possesses unitary power and authority. The constituents enjoy only delegated powers, and function as so many arms and wings of the parent body. They have neither have any independent authority nor any separate existence of their own. However, in the federal structure, the constituent organisations retain their independent status except for certain common purposes and ends. The federating body has powers and responsibilities only with regard to matters of common concern. The constituents are affiliated to the federation; and surrender their rights of independent action over a specific area or in respect of broad policies.[2] The model of organisation adopted by the AIBOC through its constitution is federal vertical structure, where fourteen officers' organisations representing different banks joined to form a federation of officers' organisation with a hierarchical structure of decision-making.[3] Thus, the constituent members of the AIBOC have their own independent identities and membership and all constituent members automatically become a member of the AIBOC on affiliation.

As discussed in the previous chapter, trade unionism among the award staff had a big impact on the officers' organisation. However, unlike most of the award staff unions, which are affiliated to some political organisation the officers' organisations remained independent of political affiliation. Like its predecessor, the AIBOC remained independent and autonomous. One of the major reasons for these officers' organisations to remain independent was because the officers believed themselves to be capable of running the organisation without outside support or interference. Even during the conflict with the AICOBOO, the involvement of people outside the banks or retired officers became an important point of conflict. Therefore, the AIBOC in its founding conference decided that only an active member of the banking industry could lead the organisation and it has remained the same to this day. The independent nature of the AIBOC makes the allegiance of its members as its only source of strength for its survival and effective functioning. In a membership centred organisation, organisational structure plays an extremely important role in binding members and leaders together. To give a firm basis to the newly formed organisation, its constitution laid down an organisational set-up for the AIBOC, which fixed the responsibilities and rights of the constituent members. It also provided a clear hierarchal division of decision-making and responsibilities.

The administrative set-up of the AIBOC consists of a central office, state units, and district units. The office-bearer of the central office was elected through the General Council, which represented all the banks and financial institutions within the territory of India. According to the constitution, all officers' organisations were to be grouped into the following broad federations:[4] State Sector Banks' Officers Federation; Private Sector Banks' Officers' Federation; Co-operative Sector Banks' Officers' Federation; Regional Rural Banks' Officers' Federation; State Sector Financial Institutions' Officers' Federation; Private Sector Financial Institutions' Officers' Federation and the Working Women's Wing. Apart from 'the Working Women's Wing', which was formed later in 2008, the basis for the formation of these federations were the sectors in which officers were working. Therefore, these federations were also called 'sectoral federations' from whom affiliate nominations are made to the General Council. An affiliate can nominate one member for every 200 primary members with a minimum of 2 nominations and a maximum of 100. The General Council, thus formed, has to elect an Executive Committee for central office for the period of three years. The Executive Committee consists of office-bearers elected by the General Council and its representative(s) nominated by (a) affiliates and (b) associate members. The office-bearers of the central office includes the following: one president; ten vice-presidents; one general secretary; ten joint general secretaries; twenty deputy general secretaries; one assistant general secretary for each unit; four secretaries and one treasurer.

The members of the Executive Committee, as directed by the Constitution should have one member for each affiliate of the State Sector Banks' Officers Federation. From Private Sector Banks' Officers' Federation, Co-operative Sector Banks' Officers' Federation, and Regional Rural Banks' Officers' Federation, there should be five, two and three representations respectively for all the affiliates put together. The State Sector Financial Institutions' Officers' Federation and Private Sector Financial Institutions' Officers' Federation should have seven and three members respectively and two members should be from the Women's Wing.[5] In addition, each associate member organisation, who are either ineligible for affiliation or for valid reasons are unable to take up affiliations, but agreed with the objectives, policies and programme of the AIBOC – can have one representative on the Executive Committee of the Confederation.

The constitution empowered the Executive Committee to implement the programmes and policies and directives of the General Council and to incorporate all such measures within the frame work of the constitution to strengthen the organisational and financial position of the confederation.[6] The Executive Committee would have to execute all the central level programmes, for which the central office is used, which is under the General Secretary assisted by other office-bearers stationed at the headquarters of the confederation. After the General Council, the Executive Committee is the second highest decision making body followed by the Working Committee, the State Council, the State Committee, the District Council, the District Committee, the City/Town Council, and at the last ladder of decision making is the City/Town Committee.[7] The Working Committee is constituted by the Executive Committee with not more than 52 members, drawn from the office-bearers which also functions at the central level.

A state unit is an administrative unit of the AIBOC, whose jurisdiction is over the entire or part of a state or union territory or over a group of states together.[8] The State/Union Territory Council consists of members nominated by affiliated organizations on the basis of one for every 100 primary members of each such organization, having their place of work within the jurisdiction of the State/Union Territory Unit shall be ex-officio members of the State Council.[9] The State Council, then, elects the State Committee, which consists of one president, one secretary, six or less vice-presidents, one treasurer, five or less organising secretaries and one assistant treasurer, one deputy secretary from each affiliated organisations and one assistant secretary from each District Unit.[10]

The district unit of the AIBOC is an administrative unit at the district level for grass-root organisation and functioning. For the administration at district level, a district committee is elected by the District Council.[11] A District Council consists of five or fewer members nominated by each affiliated organization, from amongst its primary members having their place of work within the district along with members of the State Council having their place of work within the district shall be the ex-officio members of the District Council.[12] The District Council, then, elects the District Committee consisting of one president, one secretary, two vice-presidents, one treasurer, three assistant secretaries and one assistant treasurer.[13] The procedure for the formation of City/Town Council is similar to the District Council with its place of functioning being the city/town instead of the district. The City/Town Committee is also elected in a similar manner with the exact same number of office bearers.

The organisational structure given above is as per the current constitution, which has evolved and changed over time. However, the basic idea of the organisational structure has remained intact from the first draft of the constitution. In the sections below, we take a look at how the AIBOC tried to establish the organisation envisioned in the constitution. The problems faced by them in the process of organisation building and the important amendments, which were passed by each General Council in response to those problems are also discussed here so as to give a good idea of the development of the organisation.

Development of the Organisational Structure and First General Council Meeting

The founding conference of the AIBOC elected an interim Executive Committee from the constituent members. In line with the constitutional recommendation that the 'AIBOC shall be led by serving officers only', a fourteen-member interim committee was constituted with R.N. Godbole and S.R. Sengupta elected as the founding General Secretary and President respectively. The interim committee was given the task of holding the General Council within a year. As the General Council was the highest decision making body of the organisation, it was only through the General Council that a formal committee and a formal structure could be adopted.

The interim committee was given the time-period of a year to execute the organisation model described in its constitution, as it had to hold the General Council within that period. In the founding conference itself, twenty-one convenors for the state of Gujarat, Maharashtra, Karnataka, Kerala, Tamil Nadu, Andhra Pradesh, Orissa, West Bengal, Bihar, Assam, Tripura, Manipur, Meghalaya, UP, MP, Delhi, Rajasthan, Punjab, Haryana, Himachal Pradesh, and Jammu & Kashmir were nominated. It was directed that a proper state level committee had be built within a period of 6 month and a proper election for the full-fledged state committee should be held. It was decided that the first formal Executive Committee should be held at Madras on 8 and 9 November 1985 in order to decide the further course of action and strategy to consolidate the organisation.[14]

For the formation and proper working of the organisation, the AIBOC realised the need for a regular communication with its members. Apart from sending circulars regularly, the magazine, *Common Bond,* which belonged to the All India State Bank Officers' Federation and the AICOBOO, was taken over by the AIBOC and from October 1985. From then onwards, it has become the mouthpiece of the AIBOC, publishing all the major news related to organisational development, wage negotiations and other news related to the trade union movement in India, in general and the banking and financial sector in particular. It was not just a way of providing information to members, but also as a medium to get feedback from its membership spread all across the country through the 'Letters to the Editor'.

The motive of the Confederation was to reach out to the maximum number of banks started with the its formation. Just after the foundation of the AIBOC, a rally was held at the SBI building at New Delhi, where the leaders made a decision to have a show of strength at an all-India level. In this regard, marches were held in different parts of the country. R.N. Godbole addressed a gathering of officers at Madras, S.S. Dabolkar organised a meeting of bank officers at Bombay, along with rallies and meetings in Tamil Nadu, Kerala, Gujarat, Karnataka, Punjab, Haryana, West Bengal.[15]

The first Executive Committee meeting took comprehensive note of all the issues facing the banking industry. They constituted several committees to look into certain specific matters in more detail. Some committees that were formed in this manner were: on promotion policy, transfer policy, categorisation of branches and posts and norms for provision of leased accommodation to officers and service conduct and discipline.[16] The Executive Committee also discussed the methods to strengthen the state units. In this regard, it was decided that in order to meet the immediate requirements of the state units, a fund may be constituted at the local level called the State Units' Fund (Local), which would come into existence by collecting contributions from local units of affiliates and donations from members. It was, further, instructed to the state units that an account in the name of the "All India Bank Officers' Confederation - State Unit (Local Fund)" should be opened at the state level. The president or the secretary should be authorised to operate the account jointly with the treasurer or in his/her absence with any other member of the state committee for this purpose. Meanwhile, it was also decided that measures would be taken to build up a state units' fund at the central level. In addition, an instruction was given to the state units that all the state units should take steps for establishing district units.[17]

Following the guidelines, state convenors started organising the officers in their respective states. Goa was the first to launch its unit on 22 February 1986. The General Body of the Goa state unit elected A.S. Prabhu of UCO Bank as the President and Munir A. Shaik was elected as the Secretary.[18] On 8 March 1986, the Karnataka State Unit was launched and M.J. Venkata Rao, who was the convenor of the ad-hoc committee, was elected as the President and Shantha Raju became the first Secretary of the unit. At the time of its inauguration, Karnataka unit had already organised 11 district units out of 19 districts in the state and the conference decided to organise the remaining 8 district as soon as possible.[19] The next state to launch its unit was Calcutta, which organised its first conference on 29 and 30 March 1986. Deepak Basu of the State Bank of India became the Secretary and R.R. Roy became the President.[20] In Delhi, the state unit was launched on 2 April, where Umed Singh was elected unanimously as the President and K.S. Nair as the Secretary. The Maharashtra Unit held its first conference on the 19 and 20 April 1986 at Bombay. S.S. Dadholkar of the Bank of India was elected as the Secretary and H.R. Shenoy of Syndicate Bank as the President. The conference also passed a resolution resolving to set-up units at district levels.[21] A meeting of the activists of the AIBOC was held at Bhubaneswar on 31 May 1986.[22] A conference of bank officers in the District of Giridih (Bihar) was held on 8 June 1986.[23] A meeting of the AIBOC activists was held at Bhopal on 24 June 1986. N.K. Khare of the Bank of India was elected as the General Secretary of Madhya Pradesh State Unit and S.M. Deshpande of Central Bank of

India as the President.[24] It was decided that the first state level conference would be held at the earliest. By the end of one year, state units were established in all the states, though the conventions held only in the above-mentioned states.

Apart from forming state and district level units, efforts were also made to form sectoral federations. The efforts and enthusiasm of activists along with well-negotiated bipartite settlements by the leaders attracted many officers' organisations towards the AIBOC. 'All India Allahabad Bank Officers' Association' and 'New Bank Officers' Congress' were the first ones to ask for affiliation.[25] The Executive Committee, which met at Lucknow on 7 and 8 May 1986 granted the affiliation and the General Secretary of both the organisations, K.P. Rai of Allahabad Bank and G.S. Samanta of New Bank Officers were co-opted as members of the AIBOC Executive Committee.

From the very beginning, the AIBOC had major representation from state sector banks, but efforts were made to organise officers in the private sector, the co-operative sector banks as well as in the Regional Rural Banking (RRB) Sector. The AIBOC recognised that in order to organise officers in these sectors it was important to understand their problems and raise their demands. Therefore, the founding conference prioritised the wage negotiation for officers in the private sector bank. The AIBOC could achieve a wage settlement in May 1986, which led to near parity in pay scales among officers of private and public sector banks. This attracted many officers' organisations in the private sector towards the AIBOC. Within one year, three more officers' organisations working in private sector banks joined the AIBOC.

In regards to the RRB officers, the West Bengal State Unit became the first state to organise state level associations for the RRB officers under the name of 'RRB officers' association (West Bengal)' with A.K. Jana becoming its president.[26] As a further step to organise the officers of RRBs, the Executive Committee of the AIBOC met at Bangalore on 22, 23, and 24 September 1986 set-up an Ad-hoc committee with B. Dutta Chowdhary of Sagar Grameen Bank as the convenor.[27] The committee was assigned the task to visit the RRBs in West Bengal, Bihar, Uttar Pradesh, Rajasthan, Haryana, Himachal Pradesh, Orissa and North Eastern States to set up units of the AIBOC at all possible centres. They were also instructed to work out a detailed scheme for the formation of All India RRB Officers' Federation. The committee was asked to submit a report on its activities at the next meeting of the Executive Committee scheduled to be held at Hyderabad on 15 December 1986. The ad-hoc committee started its work as instructed and collected data regarding the working conditions of RRB officers and charted out demands for them.[28]

The AIBOC also initiated the task of organising officers' in the co-operative banks. In this regard, the state unit of Maharashtra took the initiative to form a committee with A.S. Mahajan and A.V. Pandit as Joint Convenors.[29] The committee sent out circulars to officers' organisations in different co-operative banks in the state, inviting them to unite under the AIBOC and try their best to organise them. However, the West Bengal unit again became the first to organise officers in co-operative banks under the banner of 'West Bengal State Co-operative Bank Officers' Association'.

The efforts and enthusiasm of activists of the AIBOC brought many officers' organisation within its ambit. However, the period of one year was not enough to form a sectorial federation, but they could organise state and district level units majorly across the country. Bound by the decision of foundation conference, the AIBOC decided to hold the General Council on 16, 17 and 18 December 1986.[30]

The first General Council was held at Hyderabad where the rebel group of the AICOBOO first met and decided to form another organisation. A formal structure was given to the organisation in this meeting. As prescribed in the constitution, General Secretary R.N. Godbole presented the first General Secretary's report of the AIBOC. Apart from the issues faced by banks officers, the report also included national and international issues of importance. It also reported the achievements of the organisation within the period of last one year and pointed out the tasks and goals ahead. The report was then thoroughly discussed by the delegates and adopted unanimously. The General Council then elected the office bearers, S.R. Sengupta, and R.N. Godbole again became the President and Secretary of the organisation respectively. Apart from the incomplete task of deepening the organisational base, the General Council, for the next three years took up the following tasks: 100 per cent membership in the banking sector. Consolidation of the officers' movement in the private and regional rural banks, and the co-operative sectors under the banner of the AIBOC was made an objective. Another aim was the achievement of a fresh salary revision in 1987, which would be free from all anomalies and deficiencies. The General Council also adopted many resolutions related to working environment of the bank officers. The resolutions included issues of payment of bonus, security arrangements in banks, five-day week, pension among many other issues (Annexure 3).

Expanding Organisation and the Second General Council Meeting

The first General Council gave a new enthusiasm to the organisation and it geared its activities to achieve the tasks it had undertaken for itself. Immediately after the General Council, the executive committee met to decide the further course of action. The task of forming sectoral federations of the AIBOC was at the top of the list. In this regard, the ad-hoc committee for the RRB officers was instructed to enhance its base and take required steps for the formation of an All India federation for the RRB officers as soon as possible. It was also decided to hold a meeting of representatives of the AIBOC's affiliates in the private sector to set up a federation for officers of private sector banks.[31] It was also decided that the organisation base should be increased and that there should be an effort to reach out to as many banks as possible.

In this regard, the office-bearers of the organisation toured all around the country. By the first General Council, the AIBOC had already formed state units in 25 states and

2 union territories. The office bearers went to all the state units with the message to expand the organisation base.[32] The state units were directed to form the district units at the earliest. The state and district units were asked to help expand the organisational base in the private sector, the RRBs, and the co-operative sectors. The AIBOC celebrated its second foundation day on 6 October 1987 as 'Consolidation Day', and appeals were made to all bank officers and their organisations to join the AIBOC. In response to this, the All India Dena Bank Officers' Federation left the AICOBOO and joined the AIBOC. Other organisations like the Corporation Bank Officers' Organisation, the All India Vijaya Bank Officers' Association, and the Indian Overseas Bank Officers' Association also joined the AIBOC. With this, the AIBOC coverage extended to 24 public sector Banks, which constituted 85 per cent of the total officers in the banking sector.[33]

Officers of the Bank of Baroda and the Andhra Bank also approached the AIBOC for setting up an independent union, as they were dissatisfied with the existing unions in their banks. It was alleged by the officers in these two banks that management was exploiting the officers in the absence of any true trade union organisation.[34] Therefore, the AIBOC decided to launch an independent officers' organisation in both the banks. On 16 July 1989, the All India Bank of Baroda Officers' Federation (AIBOBOF) was formed in a conference at Bombay.[36] In the policy declaration, the convention stated that the All India Bank of Baroda Officers' Federation was completely committed to the path of independent trade unionism and pledged to promote and defend the rights and interests of the officers at the Bank of Baroda. The convention constituted a 16 member interim committee (with S.S. Dabholkar as the President and S.C. Rindani as the General Secretary) to carry out the functions of the federation till a duly elected committee came into being.[37]

The situation of the officers at the Andhra Bank was quite similar. The AIBOC decided to form a federation at the Andhra Bank as well, and the task was given to K. Ramakoteswara Rao and P. Veera.[37] They released an appeal to the officers of the Andhra Bank stating the need for an independent officers' organisation to fight for their rights. Many officers showed their enthusiasm for the independent organisation. Thus, on 6 August 1989, the All India Andhra Bank Officers' Federation (AIABOF) was launched at the conference held at Hyderabad, where K. Ramakoteswara Rao became the General Secretary and P. Veera Raghavan became the President. By 1996, the AIABOF became organisation with maximum number of members.[38]

In an effort to establish a sectoral federation, the ad-hoc committee for the regional rural bank officers took up the task with all seriousness. With the knowledge that the first step towards organising the RRB officers was to take up their issues. The committee developed a demand charter and submitted it to the executive committee of the AIBOC.[39] The Executive Committee, which met at Delhi on 13 and 14 June 1987, decided that the charter of demands should be submitted to the government, for the revision of the terms and conditions regarding the service of officers of the RRBs. The Executive Committee strongly advocated for parity in wages between officers of the RRBs and officers of the public sector banks. They advocated this demand on the ground of 'equal pay for equal work'. Since the work done and responsibility assumed by the RRB officers was similar to those of officers of the public sector banks; therefore, officers of the RRBs should get the same compensation for work, which officers of public sector bank received. Further, the ultimate employer in case of the RRBs as well as the public sector banks was the central government.[40]

In pursuance of the decision of the Executive Committee, the AIBOC wrote letters (Annexure 4) addressed to the chairpersons of all the regional rural banks asking parity in pay structure with the officers in nationalised banks. The letter along with the enclosed copy of the charter of demands was also sent to the National Bank for Agriculture and Rural Development (NABARD) and the banking division. Copies of the letter were also forwarded to the Prime Minister and prominent Members of Parliament. There was an all-out effort by the AIBOC to publicize their demands. Therefore, all the affiliates, state units, district units and activists were instructed to publicize the charter of demands irrespective of whether they worked in the private sector or the public sector. The AIBOC demanded that the government should create a machinery for the determination of terms and conditions for the service of officers of the RRBs through bilateral negotiations.

In the process of fighting for the parity of pay scales for the RRB officers, many organisations in the RRB got affiliated to the AIBOC. Finally, the 'All India Regional Rural Bank Officers' Federation' (AIRRBOF) was set up on 23 August 1987 at a conference held at Ranchi.[41] At that time, 20 affiliates from the RRB were attached to the AIBOC. The federation along with the state units made intensive effort to widen its coverage and were successfully able to increase its affiliation to 42, which were drawn from 17 states by the time the AIBOC concluded its second General Council.[42] The AIRRBOF decided to launch an agitation for parity in pay structure at par with the officers of the nationalised banks. However, on 26 November 1987, the government appointed a national tribunal with Justice S. Obul Reddy (a retired Chief Justice of Andhra Pradesh High Court) as the Chairperson. The tribunal looked into the matter of pay, salary, allowances and other benefits for the employees of the RRBs.[43] This move was welcomed by the AIBOC, even though it made it clear that the bipartite was the best solution for industrial relations problems. The AIRRBOF filed its statement and participated in the proceedings before the tribunal. The tribunal, which gave its award in 1990, applied the principle of parity in wages between all regional and nationalised banks.[44]

Since the AIBOC successfully secured parity for officers in private sector banks, several officers' organisations applied for affiliation with the confederation. In order to discuss the matter a meeting of representatives of the AIBOC's affiliates in the private sector was held on 1 February 1987 at Ernakulum, where it was decided that preliminary steps would be taken for the formation of 'All India Private Sector Banks Officers' Federation'. In this regard, an appeal was sent to all the officers' organisations in private sector to join the AIBOC and to strengthen the officers' movement.[45] The All India Bank of Rajasthan Officers' Association, the Karur Vysya Bank Officers' Association, the Ratnakar Bank Officers' Association and the Officers' Association of Parur Central Bank, joined the fraternity of the AIBOC. These constituted a total of nine affiliates of the AIBOC in private sector banks, which together had a majority of the officers in the private sector. With this, the task of formation of a sectoral front in private sector banks was close to its completion. The Executive Committee, which met on 13 and 14 June 1987, decided that a meeting of the general secretaries of the affiliates in the private sector banks should be held at Bangalore on 15 July 1987 to decide upon the formation of a federation in private sector banks.[46] The Executive Committee issued an appeal to all officers and officers' organisations in private sector banks, (who were outside the sphere of the AIBOC), to join the organisation and strengthen the bargaining power of the officers' movement. All these efforts successfully culminated in the formation of the 'All India Private Sector Banks' Officers' Federation' (AIPSBOF), which had 12 affiliates from the private sector banks.[47] With the given time period of one year, AIPSBOF held its first national convention, where B.L. Rathore was elected as the President and P.V. Mathew as the General Secretary.[48] Before the second General Council, AIPSBOF was able to enhance its reach even further and hence out of the total 25 private sector banks in the country, it had 15 banks within it. Thus, the AIPSBOF was representing 90 per cent of the officers in the private sector.

The organisational reach of the AIBOC was increasing in the public sector, the private sector, and the RRBs at a very fast pace. Inspired by these developments, the Executive Committee of the AIBOC decided to launch the All India Co-operative Sector Banks' Officers' Federation in its two-day session at Bangalore on 6 and 7 April 1989. At the time of its foundation, the AIBOC had only one co-operative sector officers' association, namely the West Bengal State Co-operative Bank Officers' Association. With the Bihar State Co-operative Bank Officers' Association (Patna) and the Goa Urban Co-operative Bank

Officers' Association (Panjim) joining in, the AIBOC launched All India Co-operative Sector Banks' Officers' Federation on 7 April 1989 with Ranjit Rajan Ray becoming the President and Ajoy Kumar Mukherjee as the General Secretary.[49]

All these organisational developments, along with the fifth bipartite settlement, which ensured the simultaneous date of effect as the award staff, the period between the first and the second General Council was the most fruitful for the organisation. It was during this period that the AIBOC started taking issues of officers in other financial institutions other than banks. To coordinate with the officers' associations in financial institutions, the AIBOC took initiative and officers' associations in the RBI, IDBI, UTI, NABARD, LIC, and the GIC responded positively, and this led to the formation of the 'Coordination Committee of Officers' Associations in Financial Institutions' in the April of 1987. The task of this coordination committee was to coordinate activities, particularly during the negotiation for salary revisions.[50]

All these achievements gave good reasons to the leadership of the AIBOC to go ahead with the second General Council with joy and satisfaction. Representing officers' organisations in 26 banks in the public sector, 18 banks in the private sector, 3 state level co-operative banks and 45 regional rural banks, the AIBOC celebrated its second General Council meeting on 16 to 18 December 1989 at Ahmedabad. The second General Council maintained the leadership in the secured hands of R.N. Godbole and S.R. Sengupta.[51] With the well-negotiated bipartite settlement and a well-functioning organisation, the second General Council of the AIBOC, became a place for the officers in the banking industry to think about the larger trade union movement within the country. In addition, the situation faced by the working class in India and around the world became a point of discussion. Apart from the resolutions related to the working conditions of bank officers, the Conference also passed resolutions regarding communal harmony and working class unity were also passed by the General Council (Annexure 5).

AIBOC – Then and Now

By the third General Council, which was held between 9 and 11 October 1993 at Agra, the AIBOC was able to reach out to the majority of banks and was also able to establish state level organisations in all the states. The AIBOC further reorganised the state level units to reach out to the maximum number of officers. As many states in India are quite large for one unit to look after the whole state, some unit was further bifurcated. It bifurcated many state units into different groups, like the Bihar unit was divided into Bihar (North), Bihar (South); the MP unit into MP (East), MP (West); the Maharashtra unit into Maharashtra (I), (II), (III), & (IV) and the Uttar Pradesh unit again into four zones. New units were set up for Pondicherry, Chandigarh, and Andaman & Nicobar Islands. The total state units by the third General Council reached to 36. Further, the AIBOC also established its unit in the Oriental Bank of Commerce and the Bank of Maharashtra. Even its sectorial expansion was commendable, as the coverage in the RRB sector increased by 20 units, in the co-operative sector by four units and in the private sector by one unit.[52]

With a well-established organisation in the banking industry, the AIBOC leadership now realized that there was a need for the officers in other financial institutions to be brought under organised trade unions. While working with the unions in other financial institutions under the 'Coordination Committee of Officers' Associations in Financial Institutions', the AIBOC realised that most financial institutions had either no or inactive unions. Therefore, the Executive Committee put forth the idea that the AIBOC should organise officers in other financial sector as well. The General Council considered this matter on a serious note and an amendment to the constitution was suggested. Through this amendment, the AIBOC opened its membership to officers' associations in other financial institutions. To group the affiliates of the financial sector, two more homogeneous federations were added to the constitution, i.e. the State Sector Financial Institutions' Officers' Federation and the Private Sector Financial Institutions' Officers' Federation.[53]

By the fourth General Council, many organisations in the financial sector joined the AIBOC. Also, the coverage of the AIRRBOF extended to 76 RRBs, in the private sector two more organisations namely the Tamil Nadu Mercantile Bank Officers' Association and the Kashinath Seth Bank Officers' Association joined the AIPSBOF. There were many problems related to the functioning of the organisation at state unit level. Many state units had been established, but were not functional at due to a lack of clarity regarding their role and jurisdiction. Further, some of these units were only the extended arm of the central office and were functional only at the instruction of the central office. In the fourth General Council, the role of the state and the district units was defined more clearly. The hierarchy of the central office, the state unit and the district unit was established in the constitution through the insertion of a new clause. They also brought out a book titled *Profile of State and District Units*, which contained elaborate guidelines for organising the activities of these units. In addition, the state units were given the task to acquire a building at the headquarters of each state unit, equip the offices with necessary infrastructure, and employ regular staff. All this was to give a sense of permanency to the state unit structure.[54]

The fourth General Council was also important as it was the first time that the leadership of the organisation that was about to change. R.N. Godbole, who was the General Secretary from the formation of the organisation was about to retire and could not continue because as per the constitution of the organisation only serving officers could serve as office bearers. As he left the post, S.R. Sengupta, who was the President of the organisation from the beginning, became the second General Secretary. On the recommendation of the Executive Committee, another important amendment was made to the constitution by the General Council, through which three related articles were inserted.[55] One of them was regarding the election of an honorary member, which said that

> *on the recommendation of the Executive Committee, the General Council may co-opt as honorary members, persons having a*

> *background of trade union and social activities and experience or persons with knowledge, skill, and experience in banking, economy, rural development, labour movement, education and training, and having sympathy to the officers movement, for such terms as the General Council may specify.*

The other amendment created a post of the Chairman as the constitutional head of the AIBOC. The Chairman was given 'residual powers', whose duty was to 'act in all matters, on the advice of the President and General Secretary'. The Chairman was also allowed to address the meetings of the General Council and at least one meeting of the Executive Committee in a year. The third article provided that former office bearers may be associated with the Executive Committee as chairman, patrons, advisers and consultants. Through these constitutional amendments, R.N. Godbole was made the Chairman of the organisation.

After the commencement of the fourth General Council, another important step was the organisation of women officers. Unlike earlier, when there were hardly any women workers in the banking industry, they now constituted 30 per cent of the workforce. They had become very much visible, but despite their presence and talent there were hardly any women at the top positions in banks. Recognising the fact that it is not just the management, but also the unions, which had not given adequate thought to the problems faced by women in the banking sector the Karnataka State unit of the AIBOC took the initiative to organise a seminar on women in banking at Mangalore on 10 December 1995.[56] Through this seminar, a committee of women officers was formed, which discussed the problems related to women employees in the banking industry. Through the seminar, many problems faced by women officers came to the forefront. The women officers came forward and put forth number of issues faced by them that ranged from a lack of separate washrooms in majority of bank branches, lack of crèche, extension of working day till late nights, to discrimination in the promotion decisions, among others.

The seminar further adopted resolutions to tackle the problems faced by women employees. The resolutions called for the appointment of development officers for women, whose work would be to look into various banking schemes meant for women; it also demanded longer maternity leave, reservation for women in promotion, paternity leave for men and extra-ordinary leave during sickness of dependent members of family. This seminar was the first step in organising the women employees in the banking industry. Thus, the Karnataka unit became the first unit to organise state level conventions of women officers. Later on, the Delhi and West Bengal units also organised state level conventions at their respective states. The central level women convention of the AIBOC was held at Mumbai in December 1996, where a ten-member subcommittee was formed with Bhakti Waingankar of the Bank of India, Mumbai as the Convenor.[57] The subcommittee comprised of representatives from different states. The convention called upon the state units to ensure the following: Representation of women officers in all tiers of affiliate organisations; state conventions to be held to elect women representatives in state committees; in deciding nominations, efforts to be taken to organise meetings/conventions of women officers who would decide on their representation.

The organisation of women also reflected in the change in the organisational structure of the AIBOC. There was an amendment in the constitution made in the eighth General Council held at Chandigarh between 8 and 10 March 2008, which added that women officers should be organised under the 'Working Women's Wing' of the AIBOC.[58] All these led to addition of demands related to women workers. Their participation in the union activities has since also increased. However, despite all these improvements, there is still a lack of woman participation at the leadership level. Even after 22 years of organising women workers in banks, there has not been a female President or General Secretary ever. Even among the office-bearers, the women's representation is mainly because these leaders are a part of the women' wing and not because they have risen from the ranks of the larger mainstream organisation.

The fifth General Council meeting also decided to float a forum for retired officers as there had been struggles by them for pension. As most of the retired officers during their working period were associated with the AIBOC, they did not want to join any other organisation.[59] Therefore, an organisation named the All India Bank Pensioners and Retirees Confederation (AIBPARC) was launched.[60] In order to cater to the special problems faced by the officers of the nationalised banks, another federation called the All India Nationalised Banks Officers' Federation (AINBOF) representing the members of nationalised banks was launched in 2009.[61] All these changes and developments led to the development of the organisation in all aspects of an officers' life. The post of the chairman was scrapped later and the president was made the constitutional head and the general secretary was made the executive head of the organisation.

Through all these efforts, the AIBOC succeeded in enhancing its reach in the banking industry. As shown in the Table 2, the membership strength of the AIBOC has also increased over the years. Out of a total 2,32,640 members in 1993, the AIBOC had 1,66,752, which was 71.68 per cent. Today, out of a total 3,74,295 members in the banking industry, the AIBOC has 2,75,638 members, which constitutes 73.64 per cent.

The discussion above shows how the organisation has broad-based itself on the basis of a democratic organisational structure. This has been the key to the stable leadership that the AIBOC has provided to the officers' movement. The second important feature of its organisation is the federal structure, which accords equal rights in decision making to all members and affiliates. Other conscious efforts were made to make the organisation more democratic and inclusive, such as the establishment of the Working Women's Wing and the intervention and incorporation of the regional rural banks. Similar steps were taken to include the officers in the private sector and other financial institutions to not only increase

Table 2: Membership Strength of the AIBOC and Other Officers' Organisations

Sl. No.	Name of Union	Membership	Pecentage	Membership	Pecentage	Membership	Pecentage	Membership	Pecentage	Membership	Percentage
		(as on 31st March 1993)		(as on 31st March 1994)		(as on 31st March 1995)		(as on 31st March 1997)		(as on 31st March 2017)	
1	AIBOC	166752	71.68	171416	72.85	178776	71.41	184906	72.73	275638	73.64
2	AIBOA	31431	13.51	30100	12.79	36856	14.72	38867	15.29	39305	10.50
3	INBOC	19985	8.59	19444	8.26	18418	7.36	15848	6.23	6142	1.64
4	NOBO	3267	1.40	3375	1.43	4648	1.86	4507	1.77	3892	1.04
5	Others	709	0.30	549	0.23	1417	0.57	1119	0.44	4892	1.31
6	Non-unionised/dual membership	10496	4.51	10419	4.43	10238	4.09	8973	3.53	44426	11.87
	TOTAL	232640	100	235303	100	250353	100	254220	100	374295	100

the ambit of the AIBOC but also to strengthen the internal democracy of the organisation and to increase its sensitivity towards the conditions and problems of employees in other sections of the banking and financial sector. Thus, the AIBOC sees itself as a larger part of the democratic movement and aims to instil working class consciousness within its own members.

Notes

1. P.K. Ghosh, "Structure of Trade Union Organisation," *The Economic Weekly*, March 27, 1965, 562.
2. Ibid.
3. R.N. Godbole, *Bank Officers' Movement Takes Off*, Circular No. 1 (Bangalore, Karnataka: All India Bank Officers' Confederation (AIBOC), 1985), 2.
4. *Constitution of the AIBOC (As Amended upto 10 March, 2008)* (Bangalore, Karnataka: All India Bank Officers' Confederation (AIBOC), 2008), 11.
5. Ibid., 11.
6. Ibid., 12.
7. Ibid., 14.
8. Ibid., 4.
9. Ibid., 10.
10. Ibid., 13.
11. Ibid., 4.
12. Ibid., 10.
13. Ibid., 13.
14. R.N. Godbole, *Bank Officers' Movement Takes Off*, Circular No. 1 (Bangalore, Karnataka: All India Bank Officers' Confederation (AIBOC), 1985), 4.
15. "AIBOC Activities in Full Swing," *Common Bond*, November 1985, 4.
16. R.N. Godbole, *Committees of the AIBOC*, Circular No. 7 (Bangalore, Karnataka: All India Bank Officers' Confederation (AIBOC), 1985), 1.
17. R.N. Godbole, *State Units Fund*, Circular No. 13 (Bangalore, Karnataka: All India Bank Officers' Confederation (AIBOC), 1985), 1.
18. "Inauguration of Goa Unit," *Common Bond*, May 1986, 7.
19. "Karnataka State Unit Launched," *Common Bond*, May 1986, 7.
20. "First Conference of the State Unit," *Common Bond*, June 1986, 6.
21. "Maharashtra Unit—State Conference," *Common Bond*, May 1986, 5.
22. "AIBOC Activists' Meeting at Bhubaneswar," *Common Bond*, July 1986, 7.
23. "Report from Bihar Unit," *Common Bond*, July 1986, 6.
24. "Office-bearers Elected," *Common Bond*, August 1986, 7.
25. "New Affiliates of the AIBOC," *Common Bond*, June 1986, 2.

26. "First Conference of the State Unit," *Common Bond*, June 1986, 6.
27. "R.R.B. Officers," *Common Bond*, November 1986, 7.
28. Ibid.
29. "Maharashtra Unit—State Conference," *Common Bond*, May 1986, 5.
30. "Well Done Mr. Chari," *Common Bond*, February 1987, 5.
31. "Setting up of a Federation for Officers of Private Sector Banks," *Common Bond*, February 1987, 4.
32. "Mobilization in Full Swing," *Common Bond*, April 1987, 1.
33. R.N. Godbole, "Report of the General Secretary to the 2nd Session of General Council," *Common Bond*, January 1990, 30.
34. Ibid.
35. R.N. Godbole, *New Star on the Horizon*, Circular No. 29 (Bangalore, Karnataka: All India Bank Officers' Confederation (AIBOC), 1989), 1.
36. Ibid.
37. R.N. Godbole, *Andhra Bank Officers Free Themselves*, Circular No. 28 (Bangalore, Karnataka: All India Bank Officers' Confederation (AIBOC), 1989), 1.
38. Ibid.
39. "Service Condition of R.R.B. Officers," *Common Bond*, February 1987, 8.
40. "Regional Rural Banks' Officers - Revision of Terms and Conditions of Service," *Common Bond*, August 1987, 1.
41. R.N. Godbole, "Report of the General Secretary to the 2nd Session of General Council," *Common Bond*, January 1990, 30.
42. Ibid.
43. R.N. Godbole, "Report of the General Secretary to the 2nd Session of General Council," *Common Bond*, January 1990, 23.
44. "Regional Rural Banks' Officers - Revision of Terms and Conditions of Service," *Common Bond*, August 1987, 1.
45. "AIBOC Sphere Widens – Majority Achieved in Private Sector," *Common Bond*, July 1987, 6.
46. "Private Sector Banks." *Common Bond*, September 1987, 6.
47. R.N. Godbole, *AIPSBOF Launched*, Circular No. 22 (Bangalore, Karnataka: All India Bank Officers' Confederation (AIBOC), 1988), 1.
48. "AIPSBOF," *Common Bond*, May 1989, 6.
49. "All India Co-operative Sector Banks' Officers' Federation," *Common Bond*, May 1989, 4.
50. "Co-ordination Committee Meets at Delhi," *Common Bond*, December 1987, 1.
51. R.N. Godbole, "Report of the General Secretary to the 2nd Session of General Council," *Common Bond*, January 1990, 1.
52. R.N. Godbole, *Report of the General Secretary to the 3rd Session of General Council* (Bangalore, Karnataka: All India Bank Officers' Confederation (AIBOC), 1992), 87.

53. *Amendments to Bye-laws* (Bangalore, Karnataka: All India Bank Officers' Confederation (AIBOC), 1993), 6.
54. R.N. Godbole, "Report of the General Secretary to the 4th Session of General Council," *Common Bond*, July 1995, 27.
55. Ibid., 3.
56. "Seminar on Women in Banking," *Common Bond*, January 1996, 1.
57. S.R. Sen Gupta, "Report of the General Secretary to the 5th Session of General Council," *Common Bond*, January 1999, 29.
58. "Report of the General Secretary to the 4th Session of General Council," *Common Bond*, July 1995, 27.
59. K.V. Acharya (Current President of AIBPARC), interviewed by Sarika Chaudhary, New Delhi, India, November 2017.
60. "All India Bank Officers' Confederation – 8th Triennial General Council," *Common Bond*, April 2008, 20.
61. Harvinder Singh (Former General Secretary of the AIBOC), interviewed by Sarika Chaudhary, Bangalore, India, June 2018.

3

Struggles for Better Working Conditions

The discussion in previous chapters has shown that the opposition to the unilateral implementation of the Pillai Committee Recommendations (PCR) under the leadership of the AICOBOO forced the government and the IBA to consider the opinions of the officers' unions. Thus, there was a structuring of collective bargaining in the form of bipartite negotiations and this made the struggles for salaries and working conditions formal, and the role of unions and their leaders became extremely important. The bipartite negotiations are one of the most important component of the unions' functioning in the banking sector. There have been constant efforts by the AIBOC to secure better working conditions for the bank officers. It has been a part of every bipartite negotiations, which were held between the officers' organisations and the Indian Banks' Association. This chapter analyses in detail those negotiations and struggles led by the AIBOC in securing better working conditions and wage payment for the officers. It also demonstrates the strength of the collective bargaining power of the Confederation.

Working Conditions of Officers and the Need for Standardisation

The first chapter has shown that the working conditions of officers were quite harsh during 1960s and 1970s. The salary structure for officers working in the banking sector was arbitrarily fixed by individual bank managements. The pay scale, dearness allowance, house rent allowance along with other employment remunerations differed from bank to bank.[1] The working hour of officers used to extend till midnights. There were no causal leave available to them. Even in the case of emergency, the officers were not allowed to take leave. The salary structure introduced in different banks, had many anomalies. Officers working at two different places drawing the same salary were placed at a different basic pay. The salary scales had many problems and wrought injustices to officers. The bank level struggles had started in different parts of the country. In this respect, the 1969 indefinite strike by the officers of the State Bank of India was the milestone in the history of officers' movement. It had brought the harsh working conditions faced by bank officers in front of the larger society. Inspired by this strike, officers in other banks started organising themselves.

At the same time, 14 banks were nationalised; however, the discrepancy in the wage structure of different banks existed. This discrepancy also put forth a difficulty for the Banking Commission (1972) under the Chairpersonship of R.G. Saraiya. The commission recommended that there should be a centralised recruitment of officers for the 14 nationalised banks and therefore, a National Banking Service Commission should be set up.[2] However, they realised that the Banking Commission could not function till the anomalies in the pay structure of officers persisted. Hence, the Saraiya Commission suggested that the pay scales and other service conditions of the officers in the nationalised banks should be standardised and the government should be the one to take a lead in this direction. Therefore, a committee called the 'Committee for Standardisation of Pay Scales, Allowances and Perquisites of Officers in the Nationalised Banks' was appointed in the year 1973 under the chairpersonship of Professor U.R. Pillai,[3] by whose name the committee is popularly known as the Pillai Committee. The committee submitted its report to the government in a record time of ten months on 30 May 1974.

However, the unilateral imposition of Pillai Committee was opposed by the bank officers. It was only through bank level negotiations that Pillai Committee was implemented. The PCR were made applicable to the State Bank of India (SBI), its subsidiaries and 14 nationalised banks. The new pay scales were made applicable from 1 January 1979 and later on 1 January 1983 for the other six banks, which were nationalised later and brought under the ambit of the PCR. With the implementation of the Pillai Committee Report, there was a standardisation of the pay scale and other working conditions. This uniform wage structure brought a degree of consistency among all bank officers.

Pillai Committee Recommendations (PCR) and Its Impact

The implementation of PCR was a major event in the history of bank officers' movement and formed the basis for further negotiations. The principles taken into consideration by the Pillai Committee in the determination of pay scale were: first, that there should be an equal pay for equal work and second, that the pay scales should be related to functions and responsibilities.[4] The aim of the Pillai Committee was to standardise the pay scales and its jurisdiction was limited to officers in the 14 nationalised banks. The following were the terms of reference of the committee:[5] (a) The principles that should govern the structure of pay scales of officers of nationalised banks and to suggest such changes in the existing structure as may be necessary to bring about the standardisation of scales of pay. In making recommendations, the Committee would take into consideration the terms and conditions of the Chairman and Managing Directors of nationalised banks; (b) the allowances, amenities, facilities or benefits in kind that should be admissible to the various grades of officers in the nationalised banks; (c) the age of superannuation and the nature and quantum of terminal benefits for the other cadres; (d) principles that should govern the question of transferability of senior staff amongst the various posts which involve control over branches in policy decisions or which carry at the beginning of the scale total emoluments including perquisites of Rs. 2,000 and above per month; and (e) any other matter incidental or ancillary to the forgoing which the Committee may deem fit.

The final recommendations, (implemented in the year 1979), divided the officers into four standardised grades of top executive, senior management, middle management and junior management on the basis of identifying their broad levels of responsibility where each grade had one or more scale (see Table 1).[6] The top executive grade included all executives under the managing director such as the general manager, the joint general managers, and the deputy general managers. The senior management grade included assistant general managers and heads of functional departments in the head office of the bank. The middle management grade comprised of managers of larger and medium branches. The junior management included all other officers like managers of small branches and pay officers and accountants.[7] A standardised pay scale was attached to each standardised grade. The minimum basic pay for officers in the junior management grade was fixed at Rs. 700 per month, which was on par with comparable categories in other government sectors. It was also recommended that the standardised pay structure including the set of allowances and perquisites recommended by them should be implemented as a 'package' from an appointed date.

Pillai Committee also laid out a clear guidelines regarding appointments, probations, confirmations, promotional seniority, retirements and termination. The period of probation for the directly recruited junior officers was two years, which may be extended by one year in the case of probationers deemed unsatisfactory.[8] To ensure the development of officers within the industry, a promotion policy was also laid down and 25 per cent of the vacancies in the higher grades were reserved for the provision of accelerated promotions for the meritorious. The officers in the junior management grade were made eligible for merit promotion to scale II in the middle management grade. It was required of them to fulfil 7 years of service and pass in both parts of the Certified Associate of Indian Institute of Bankers (CAIIB)[9] or 10 years of service and a pass in part I of the CAIIB or 12 years of service. Officers with 10 years of service in the middle management grade would be eligible for promotion to the senior management grade. Officers with 5 years of service or more were deemed eligible for the election to the top executive grade.[10] In addition, there were rules highlighted by the Pillai Committee regarding fitment on promotion, allowances and perquisites, leaves and other benefits.

AIBOC and the Bipartite Negotiations

As discussed in the previous chapters, the right to negotiate was very valuable to the officers' unions. Therefore, instead of accepting whatever the government was providing to the officers, they secured their right to participate in bipartite negotiations with the Indian Banks' Association (IBA) to decide their wages. From the very beginning, they were in favour of standardisation, but mere standardisation was not enough and a revision of pay scales was required to solve outstanding problems and discrepancies. Nonetheless, the Pillai Committee became the basis of bipartite negotiations.

Initially, the jurisdiction of the Pillai Committee was limited to nationalised banks as can be found in its terms of reference. However, after the Pillai Committee submitted its report and it was decided to implement it, the government proposed that the State Bank of India should also be brought under Pillai Committee. This led to an opposition from the officers in the SBI as they did not depose in front of the Pillai Committee and their unique problems were not reflected in the Pillai Committee. Therefore, it was not easy to implement Pillai Committee as the State Bank had different scales. The bipartite negotiation between the State Bank management and the All India State Bank Officers' Federation (AISBOF) happened in the early days of 1985, which finally led to a conclusion on 18 April 1985 on how the existing scales of SBI should be made equal to Pillai Committee. However, it was not implemented until May 1986, which forced the AISBOF to go for an agitation demanding following issues: (a) Scales I to IV same as in nationalised banks; (b) Scale IV-A to be abolished; (c) Scales V to VII to be the same as in nationalised banks; (d) Special scales to be provided for CGMS and DMDs; (e) Officers in existing scales IV-A, V and VI were to be placed in new scales V, VI and VII respectively.[11] Finally, AISBOF could retain some additional facilities including four increments for probationary officers at the entry level.

With all the negotiations along with protests and strikes, it took around two years for the equalisation of scales.[12] But, private sector banks were not a part of Pillai Committee and their terms and conditions of service were arbitrarily decided by the respective managements. This led to a huge difference in the service conditions of officers in the private sector and the public sector. Therefore, the founding conference of the AIBOC set for themselves the settlement of terms and conditions of service of officers of private sector banks as their first priority.[13] The first Executive Committee meeting of the AIBOC, which was held at Madras on 8 and 9 November 1985 discussed all the pending issues and salary structure of private sector banks at length.[14] They formulated their stand and strategy for achieving parity in the terms and conditions of service amongst bank officers of both public and private sector banks. A committee led by S.R. Sengupta was constituted to conduct the negotiations with the IBA. As the first bipartite meeting between the IBA and the AIBOC on this subject was to be held on 29 and 30 November 1985 at Bombay,[15] the committee met on 27 November and a memorandum was submitted to the IBA. Thereafter, many meetings and negotiations were held and finally a settlement was reached in May 1986. Thus, a near parity in pay scales among the officers of private sector and public sector banks was achieved. This proved a boost for the confidence of private sector bank officers in the AIBOC and more and more private bank unions joined the AIBOC, and on 17 June 1987, the AIBOC secured a majority in the coverage of private sector banks.[16]

In 1984, the signing of the Joint Note by the AIBOC as 'Other Bank Officers' Organisations' and the AICOBOO representing officers and the IBA representing bankers paved the way for the first bipartite negotiations of officers.[17] By that time, three bipartite settlements were signed by award staff unions. Thereafter, there have been regular bipartite negotiations between the IBA and the officers' associations for the wage settlement. Initially the salary revision used to take place once in four years and which then became for the interval of five years. The approval of the finance minister had become mandatory for every change. All these bureaucratic works usually lead to a delay in the finalisation of the wage settlement. Generally, settlements are signed after two to two and half years of the due date, that too after many strikes called by unions for early settlement of negotiations. From the time of implementation of the Pillai Committee Recommendations until the settlement of the 10th bipartite settlement, there have been many improvements in wages for officers. The following section discusses the role played by the AIBOC in ensuring better pay scales and other emoluments for the officers.

Although the formation of the AIBOC was formally announced on 6 October 1985, their struggle and contribution in the improvement of working conditions of bank officers started much before that. The officers, who were not satisfied with the AICOBOO's method of handling negotiations, started their own negotiations with the IBA. As discussed in the previous chapter, they were able to ensure that the date of effect of the first bipartite was held on 1 February 1984 even though the IBA wanted it on 1 July 1984.[18] After its formation, the AIBOC was recognised as the principal bargaining agent on behalf of the bank officers and was allotted with six representatives, which were allotted to the AICOBOO earlier. This implies that six representatives of the AIBOC could participate in negotiations with the IBA and their travelling expenses for their participation in meetings would be reimbursed by the IBA. Other officers' confederations like the All India Bank Officers' Association (AIBOA) and the Indian National Bank Officers' Congress (INBOC) were allotted with five representatives each.

Thereafter, the AIBOC has been in the forefront of struggles to secure better wages structure for officers. Subsequently, the representation has been restricted to two for the AIBOC and one for other officers' organisations. The following section discusses the different components of pay structure as defined by the Pillai Committee and the improvements that were secured in the successive bipartite negotiations until the tenth bipartite.

Pay Structure

Basic pay is the main salary, which an employee gets from the employer before any reduction or increase. After fixing the basic pay, allowances such as dearness allowance, house rent allowance among others are added to it, and then deductions such as professional tax, income tax, contributions to provident fund etc. are made. The Pillai Committee attached one pay scale to each grade/scale. The pay structure according to PCR was as follows:

Table 3: The Pay Structure as suggested by Pillai Committee

Grade	*Scale*	*Bask Pay (Pillai Committee)*	*10th Bipartite*
Top Executive	VII	3000-125-3500	76520-2120-85000
	VI	2750-125-3250	68680-1960-76520
Senior Management	V	2500-100-2700	59170-1650-62470-1800-66070
	IV	2000-100-2400	50030-1460-55870-1650-59170
Middle Management	III	1800-75-2250	42020-1310-48570-1460-51490
	II	1200-70-1550-75-2000	31705-1145-32850-1310-45950
Junior Management	I	700-40-900-50-1100 EB 1200-60-1800	23700-980-30560-1145-32850-1310-42020

The interpretation of the above basic pay goes like this: the initial basic pay for junior management grade scale I was

Rs. 700 with an annual increment of Rs. 40 up to the time it reaches Rs. 900. Then the annual increment is Rs. 50 until the basic pay reaches Rs. 1,100 and so on. After the implementation of PCR, the pay for each of the scales have been revised regularly through bipartite negotiations.

The first problem faced by officers with regard to pay structure was related to the efficiency bar proposed by PCR. It was found that in many cases an officer, who had already crossed the efficiency bar, was once again confronted with another bar. This problem was solved after the fourth-bipartite settlement itself, when the efficiency bar was removed from the pay scale.[19] In addition, most of the officers from the fourth bipartite itself wanted the date of effect of wage settlement to be simultaneous with the award staff. However, this could not be achieved then because of the unorganised and divided unions. Learning from the last experience, the AIBOC submitted its charter of demands for the second bipartite on 22 June 1987 as the first settlement was about to expire on 30 June 1987. The IBA wanted the officers' organisations to wait till some understanding was achieved between the IBA and the employees' unions, but the AIBOC was determined to finish negotiations early this time. Therefore, the secretariat, which met at Bangalore in August 1987, decided to launch an action immediately. This created pressure on the IBA and the negotiations on salary revision started on 8 September 1987. Unfortunately, the talks between the IBA and the employees' unions entered into a stalemate on issues like the DA formula, incremental pattern among others and some of the unions that were not invited for the bipartite talks went to court. The court ordered a stay on the talks. This therefore, caused a delay but eventually talks were resumed in June 1988.[20] Once the negotiation started, the employees' unions were able to finalise an agreement on 3 December 1988, but the talks with the officers' organisations were inconclusive. The AIBOC was all prepared to go for a strike; however, the IBA had a meeting with the AIBOC and discussed certain issues, and assured that the salary revision would be discussed in the next meeting. Despite the assurance the matter of salary revision was delayed, which ultimately forced the AIBOC to go ahead with agitation. The Action Committee, which met at Bombay on 24 December 1988, called for a one-day strike on 25 January 1989 and a Dharna (sit-in) at Delhi on 31 January. After the strike protest, the government asked the Chief Labour Commissioner (Central) to intervene. Since, the officers were considered as managerial workers, they were not covered under the Industrial Dispute Act, thus, even the labour commissioner could not prove to be of much assistance. Hence, the AIBOC announced its next programme of action of strike on 28 February and a prolonged strike in the last week of March. However, the AIBOC did not require to go for a strike as the bipartite meeting at Bombay from 22 to 24 February 1989 proved to be fruitful and understandings were reached on major issues like DA, automatic upgradation in the pay scale and date of effect. The wage revision talks between the AIBOC and the IBA finally concluded on 8 March 1989. On 10 April, the fifth bipartite agreement was signed. Soon thereafter, the IBA sought the clearance of the government for signing the minutes of the agreement and finally, the agreement was signed on 11 June 1989 to give effect to the new wage settlement effective from 1 November 1987, which was simultaneous with the award staff.[21] Thus, apart from a general improvement in the pay scale, the fifth bipartite settlement also ensured a running scale and automatic movement from scale I to scale II and scale II to scale III. In addition, the problems of stagnation for junior officers had been taken care of from the monetary angle as officers in scale I and II could draw the increments of the next scale after reaching the top of the scale. Thus, the fifth-bipartite pay scale became the structure of upcoming pay scales. The table below shows the revised scales of pay specified against each bipartite settlement.

The fifth-bipartite salary revision was operative up to 1 November 1992 and the cost of this revision was 14.5 per cent. For the sixth-bipartite salary revision, a similar cost was expected by the bank officers. Meanwhile, a settlement on pension scheme and an agreement on one-time increment for computerisation, which cost an additional 6 and 3 per cent

Table 4: Pay Scales Revised in Each Bipartite Settlement

Grade	*Scale*	*4th Bipartite*	*5th Bipartite*	*6th Bipartite*	*7th Bipartite*	*8th Bipartite*	*9th Bipartite*	*10th Bipartite*
Top Executive	VII	4100-125-4600	6400-150-7000	12650-300-13250-13600-400-14000	19340-420-20180-520-20700-600-21300	29340-680-30700-900-31600-1000-32600	46800-1300-52000	76520-2120-85000
	VI	3850-125-4350	5950-150-6550	11450-300-12650	17660-420-19340	26620-680-29340	42000-1200-46800	68680-1960-76520
Senior Management	V	3575-110-3685-115-3800	5350-150-5950	10450-250-11450	16140-380-17680	24140-620-26620	36200-1000-38200-1100-40400	59170-1650-62470-1800-66070
	IV	2925-105-3450	4520-130-4910-140-5350	8970-230-9200-250-10450	13900-340-14240-380-16140	20480-560-21040-620-24140	30600-900-34200-1000-36200	50030-1460-55870-1650-59170
Middle Management	III	2650-100-3250	4020-120-4260-130-4910	8050-230-9200-250-9700	12540-340-14240-380-15000	18240-560-21040-620-22280	25700-800-29700-900-31500	42020-1310-48570-1460-51490

(Contd.)

Table 4: Pay Scales Revised in Each Bipartite Settlement (*Contd.*)

Grade	*Scale*	*4th Bipartite*	*5th Bipartite*	*6th Bipartite*	*7th Bipartite*	*8th Bipartite*	*9th Bipartite*	*10th Bipartite*
	II	1825-100-2925	3060-120-4260-130-4390	6210-230-8740	9820-340-13560	13820-500-14320-560-19920	19400-700-20100-800-28100	31705-1145-32850-1310-45950
Junior Management	I	1175-60-1475-70-1895-EB-95-2275-100-2675	2100-120-4020	4250-230-4940-350-5290-230-8050	7100-340-12540	10000-470-12820-500-14320-560-18240	14500-600-18700-700-20100-800-25700	23700-980-30560-1145-32850-1310-42020

respectively, was also proposed. Therefore, the IBA remained stubborn and claimed that the banks could not bear the further burden of 14 to 15 per cent of salary revision. Hence, the sixth bipartite settlement, which was signed on 23 June 1995, the cost of settlement was agreed as 10.5 per cent. This led to a double increase in the basic pay for a majority of the officers.

The negotiation for the seventh bipartite was about to start in 1997, and the officers' unions were ready with the charter of demands by July. However, along with the continuation to privatisation and the anti-labour policies that were being introduced in the country, the IBA tried to enforce bank level negotiations based on productivity and profitability, but it was made clear by the UFBU that wage revisions for employees and officers must be as before at an industry level only. Although the bipartite negotiations remained at an industry level, the IBA tried different methods to dodge the demands put forth by unions. It made excuses like 'banking industry passing through very critical times'; mergers of banks and retrenchment were in the offing, cut in wages in many industries had been accepted by the workers, bank balance sheets were worse, and banks had a huge surplus staff, etc. The IBA claimed that only 8 per cent of the overall wage load would be borne by banks. The IBA reiterated the same position in the negotiations that took place on 8 January 1999 between five award staff unions and four officers' associations. The unions and associations firmly rebutted the above arguments of the IBA, and told them categorically that the offer of 8 per cent wage load was unacceptable, and insisted for a negotiated settlement. The IBA did not respond positively and the United Forum of Bank Unions (UFBU)[22] went on a strike on 12 January. In the context of the unreasonable and obstinate standpoint of the IBA, the UFBU took the decision to go on an indefinite strike from 17 March 1999, preceded by a two-day's strike on 25 and 26 February 1999. In the meanwhile, the UFBU team met the Union Finance Minister, and convinced him about the charter of demands. He appealed to the UFBU leadership to go back to the negotiation table, so the negotiated settlement took place. The two days' strike demanded that: (a) there should be a uniform settlement for all banks (b) a wage load of 10 per cent (c) that the revision could be effective from 01.11.1997, but with the phasing of arrears payment. With all the strike and show of strength, the UFBU forced the IBA to sign a memorandum of understanding (MoU) with the UFBU on 11 March 1999. It was first time that an industry level tripartite MoU was signed. The IBA agreed to give effect to the settlement from 1 November 1997, subject to phasing over of the load and the overall total load to be 12.25 per cent including the cost of superannuation benefits, of the wage bill of the year ending 31 March 1997. Thus, the seventh bipartite negotiation was important as apart from securing improvement in wages, it also secured that the process of negotiation keep happening, defeating the IBA's intention to go for bank level negotiations.

For the eighth-bipartite negotiations, the four officers' organisations submitted a charter of demands for revision of wages and other service conditions for officers on 15 June 2002. The IBA invited the officers' unions for the first round of the bipartite on 18 October 2002, but the date of the bipartite meeting was postponed to 25 October, where it was decided to form a small committee for the purpose of resumption of negotiations on the charter of demands. Finally, the first round of discussion happened on 30 December 2002. In the next round of negotiation, which happened on 18 February 2003, the IBA indicated that in the light of the current trends of profit and the interest rates worsening, the industry could not bear the burden of wage revision as demanded. The AIBOC suggested that the IBA should come out with a fair and reasonable offer to enable the officers' organisations to respond favourably. Again, a meeting was held between the committee of the IBA and representatives of the officers' organisations on 12 March. In that meeting, the IBA agreed that they would examine the proposals of the AIBOC as regards the issue of a running scale, integration of the existing scales of II and III and IV and V, and a 100 per cent neutralisation of the DA. However, the IBA did not do anything even after having another meeting on 3 April. Finally, tired of the slow pace of negotiations, the AIBOC gave a call for a strike on 2 May. The UFBU also decided on a joint struggle to ensure early wage revision within a fixed time frame. The IBA convened a bipartite meeting on 25 July, but that too failed. Finally, in the meeting held on 26 December, the IBA offered 8.8 per cent as wage increase, but this was rejected by the officers' organisation as it was far below the expectation of 20 per cent. The IBA agreed to convene the next meeting by the middle of January 2004 and to resume negotiations. This slow and frustrating salary negotiation led the UFBU to go on a strike on 24 April 2004. The negotiation resumed on 19 April 2004, where the AIBOC presented their views. The IBA assured a flexible approach and also indicated that a MoU could be signed in the month of May. Thereafter, there were many meeting between the unions and the IBA, and many issues were discussed. One of them was performance related incentive schemes to which the unions expressed their open-mindedness but added that it could be only introduced after a reasonable and fair wage revision and that there could be no dilution of the industry level settlement. After this, many issueswere discussed like the per centage increase in wages, DA, pension. After the meeting held on 2 September 2004, which ended up in a stalemate, the UFBU went on an agitation against the IBA's attitude. They went on a strike on 24 August 2004 and decided to go for a strike on 5 and 6 October, but the Chief Labour Commissioner (Central) intervened and there were improvements made in the negotiations. On the meeting held on 7 December 2004, a wage increase by 13.25 per cent was achieved.

The officers' organisations and workers' unions under the banner of the United Forum of Bank Unions submitted the charter of demands to the chairperson of the IBA on 29 October 2007 in connection with the salary revision due from 1 November 2007. The chairperson of the committee assured the workers organisations that the negotiations will commence at the right time and expressed his desire to ensure a speedy settlement. The major demand taken up by the unions was the availability of a second option in pension and a few meetings were held exclusively for salary revision. The IBA initially in the meeting held on 21 January 2009 made an offer of Rs. 2,750

Crores, which was around 10 per cent increase in the wage cost, but this offer was rejected by the AIBOC and emphasised the need for a substantial increase in the offer made by the IBA. After a discussion held on 12 February, the IBA offered an increase in wage of Rs. 3,600 Crores for the employees and officers put together, but the AIBOC once again rejected the offer insisting for maintaining external parity and better salary package. In the next meeting held on 21 February 2009, the IBA informed that they did not have a mandate to go beyond the earlier offer of Rs. 3,600 Crores and hence could not improve their offer any further. Thereafter, it was decided that unions would meet and submit a memorandum to the Finance Minister, the Labour Minister, the Chairmen of the IBA and the negotiating committee. After the meeting with the ministers, there was another meeting on 11 May 2009, where the IBA improved their offer to Rs. 4,125, i.e., an increase of 15 per cent over the wage bill. However, even this offer fell short of the demand of the 20 per cent increase in wage bill; hence, the UFBU rejected the offer of the IBA. The UFBU then decided to go for a strike on 12 June. Before they could go ahead with the strike, the IBA called the UFBU for a bipartite meeting on 9 June, where it was agreed that wage bill would be increased by 17 per cent and hence, the UFBU deferred the proposed strike on 12 June. However, the IBA went back to its offer of 17 per cent increase and reiterated that they could not increase it beyond 15 per cent. This led to a wide spread anger among the members of UFBU, thus, they decided to go for a two-day strike on 6 and 7 August 2009. The Chief Labour Commissioner (Central) intervened in the matter and directed the IBA to negotiate with the UFBU on 4 August. That meeting with the IBA was a shock to the UFBU as the IBA said that they could offer only a 13 per cent wage increase. This was unacceptable to the union members; they decided to go ahead with the strike. Consequently, the government instructed the Chief Labour Commissioner to hold a conciliatory meeting between the UFBU and the IBA. In this conciliatory meeting held on 7 August 2009, the IBA offered an increase of 17.5 per cent in wage fund. This offer was accepted by the UFBU, and thus, the ninth bipartite settlement was signed on 27 April 2010, where the annual wage increase was Rs. 4,816 Crores (Rs. 2,239 Crores for officers and Rs. 2,577 Crores for employees).

The ninth bipartite settlement was about to end on 31 October 2012, therefore, the award staff unions and officers' organisations had collectively prepared comprehensive common charter of demands after threadbare discussions amongst themselves. The practice over the last three bipartite meetings was that the constituents of the United Forum of Bank Unions would call the IBA and submit the charter of demands, which was once again followed. The UFBU sought an appointment with the chairperson of the IBA to submit their common charter of demands. The meeting took place on 30 October 2012, where the UFBU submitted the charter of demands.[23] It was expected by the UFBU that the negotiations would resume on time and the settlement could be reached early. On 22 February, a preliminary round of discussions took place between the IBA and the UFBU. Both sides felt and agreed that the negotiations should be expedited and concluded in a time bound manner.[24] The next round of talks was to be held on 4 March 2013.[25] However, the meeting was postponed.[26] The second round of discussions happened on 22 April, exactly two months after the preliminary discussions.[27] The UFBU conveyed its unhappiness over the manner in which the negotiations were held and expressed their concerns for an early salary revision. In that meeting, the IBA came out with proposals like introduction of cost to company method of wage payment, introduction of performance linked variable pay and restriction on applicability of wage revision.

These demands of management were totally unacceptable to the unions as it challenged the very foundation of bipartite relations. After this meeting, it was clear to the unions that the attitude of the IBA was confrontational rather than cooperative. Therefore, the UFBU went for a protest action and called for a strike for 48 hours from 20 January. In this regard, the Chief Labour Commissioner called the representatives of the UFBU and the IBA for a conciliation meeting on 13 January 2014, where it was decided the parties would be meeting again on

17 January. In the negotiation meeting held on 17 January 2014, the IBA offered an increased wage bill from 5 per cent to 9.5 per cent. These improvements in the offer and assurance of further advancement showed a change in attitude of the IBA and led the UFBU to defer its strike. The next negotiation, which happened on 27 January 2014, the wage bill was increased only by 0.5 per cent and it was made clear by IBA that 10 per cent, was the last offer. This again generated anger amongst unions and they decided have a two-day strike on 10 and 11 February 2014. Once again the Chief Labour Commissioner intervened and a conciliation meeting was held on 6 February, where the commissioner and the IBA reiterated the same offer and requested the UFBU to accept the offer and consider it as a result of bipartite. However, the UFBU made it clear that the 10 per cent increase offered by the IBA was not unacceptable and thus, they went ahead with the strike. Again a meeting was held between the IBA and the UFBU, where both the parties gave arguments supporting their demands. The IBA stated that profitability of banks do not allow them to improve the wages in further, whereas the UFBU showed the recommendations of the Seventh Pay Commission, to insist that there was a huge gap between the pay scale of bank employees and government employees in comparable jobs and therefore, a substantial increase in the wage was a must.

The next round of negotiations took place only after three months on 13 June 2014 owing to the general elections. In this meeting, The IBA informed the unions that they were willing to improve the wage bill from 10 to 11 per cent. However, the UFBU refused to accept this offer and informed that their minimum expectation was a 25 per cent increase in the pay slip. To this, the IBA expressed its inability to accept the same as it was beyond the paying capacity of the banks. The UFBU then wrote letters to the newly elected Prime Minister and the Finance Minister stating their demands and the arguments for the justification. Therefore, there were two further rounds of wage revision talks on 17 September and 26 September 2014, where some issues like 100 per cent DA neutralisation on pension for the officers retired before November 2002, and

100 per cent reimbursement of hospitalisation cost incurred were discussed among others. However, the IBA was adamant on the wage bill and claimed that they could not increase it beyond 11 per cent. Therefore, the UFBU decided to go on a protest action programme from 10 to 31 October 2014. Different protest programmes were undertaken, for example the wearing of black badges, country wide protest demonstrations, one day dharna (sit-in) at all state capitals, and a nationwide one day protest strike. Again, the Central Labour Commissioner intervened, but that did not help the issue. Thus, the UFBU decided to strike on 12 November 2014. Thereafter, there were other action programmes taken up by the UFBU like the relay zonal strikes, rallies and protests, which culminated into a march to parliament on 9 December 2014. The representatives of different unions met the Prime Minister Narendra Modi and submitted their memorandum. Once again, no heed was paid to the demands of unions, and therefore, they decided to continue their struggle. In this direction, a candle light march was organised on 16 December 2014 in all state capitals. Again, at the call of the Chief Labour Commissioner (CLC), one more round of conciliation was held at 17 December 2014, but the IBA stuck to 11 per cent wage bill. Therefore, the UFBU decided to go for a strike on 7 January 2015. Once again, a conciliation meeting by the CLC was held on 5 January, where the IBA offered an increase in the pay bill to 12.5 per cent but this was not accepted by the UFBU. There were few more meetings and strike notices, which ultimately led to a 15 per cent increase in wage bill.[28] Hence, after a clearance from the ministry of finance the tenth bipartite settlement was signed on 25 May 2015.[29] Another major achievement of the tenth bipartite settlement was the declaration of the second and the fourth Saturday as a holiday in the banking industry.[30]

Today the banking sector is in the middle of eleventh bipartite talks. The officers' organisations have submitted their charter of demands to the IBA on 5 June 2017, where they reminded the management that the Pillai Committee Recommendations were implemented to ensure parity in wages within banking system and with the civil servants. However, from 1992 onwards, there has been a disparity among the wages of officers in banking sector and central government officers groups A.[31] Therefore, the unions have demanded a parity among the two and the principles of the Seventh Pay Commission should be applicable to bank officers with the retention of the right of negotiation and participation in wage determination.

Dearness Allowance

The Dearness Allowance (DA) is a cost of living adjustment allowance. DA is calculated as a per centage of basic pay to mitigate the impact of inflation. The Pillai Committee adopted the principle of 75 per cent neutralisation of the increase in the cost of living up to a salary level of Rs. 900 per month. Officers up to this level were made eligible for quarterly adjustments in the DA for every rise or fall of 8 points above 200 points in the quarterly average of the All India Average Working Class Consumer Price Index (hereafter AIWCCPI) (1,960 = 100). The rate of adjustment for every rise of 8 point in the quarterly average of the index was fixed at 3 per cent of the basic pay for the officers in the salary range above Rs. 900 per month. For the officers in the salary range of Rs. 901 to Rs. 1,600 per month, the first adjustment was made only after 16 points; and for salary range above Rs. 1,601, it was only after 24 points. Above that, there was a ceiling, according to which the salary plus DA could not exceed beyond Rs. 2,400 per month.

For the fifth bipartite settlement, the AIBOC demanded the abolition of the ceiling on DA. This demand was accepted by the IBA, thus, the ceiling of DA was abolished. The unrealistic cycle of 8, 16 and 24 points rise or fall of the CPI was also replaced by quarterly increase or decrease. When the AIBOC was in the middle of the talks on residuary issues, which began on 20 October 1989, a new dimension was given to the wage structure by the RBI in its settlement. In the package agreed and implemented by RBI assured that the DA formula was based on: 100 per cent neutralisation for basic pay range up to Rs. 2,500; 75 per cent neutralisation for pay range between Rs. 2,501 and

Rs. 4,000 and 50 per cent for pay above Rs. 4,000. As against this, in the banking industry the formula was based on: 100 per cent neutralisation up to Rs. 1,650 of pay; 75 per cent for pay range of Rs. 1,651 and Rs. 2,836; 50 per cent neutralisation for pay range of Rs. 2836 and Rs. 4,020 and 25 per cent neutralisation for pay beyond Rs. 4,020. The AIBOC submitted a memorandum and demanded the introduction of the RBI pattern DA for Bank Officers as well. Ultimately, on 18 April 1990 the IBA agreed to DA parity of bank officers with the RBI officers. The new DA formula was implemented with effect from 1 November 1987.

In the charter of demand for the seventh bipartite settlement, the officers' organisations demanded that there should be a monthly adjustment of the DA along with 100 per cent neutralisation uniformly at all stages. Although the first demand could never be fulfilled, but during the eighth bipartite the second demand came for consideration. The IBA agreed to the 100 per cent DA neutralisation and it was made applicable to all future payments with effect from 1 February 2005. Today after the tenth bipartite settlement, the DA is payable at 0.10 per cent for every rise or fall of four points over 4,440 points in the quarterly average of the All India Average Working Class Consumer Price Index base 1,960 = 100.

Residential Accommodation and House Rent Allowance (HRA)

One of the disadvantages brought about by PCR was with respect to HRA. The Pillai Committee discontinued with practice of providing free house to officers and made it clear that officers should not be entitled to residential accommodation by the bank as a matter of right. Instead, it was made open to the banks to decide about the provision of residential accommodation. It was further added that if officers were provided with residential accommodation, they would have to pay 10 per cent of the pay or the standard rent, whichever is less. It was further added, whenever residential accommodation is provided by banks, electricity, water, gas and other conservancy charges should be paid by the officers concerned and not by the bank.

House Rent Allowance (HRA) is paid to all officers not provided with accommodation by the bank. For the payment of HRA, the Pillai Committee recommended that the place of work should be divided into four categories of Major 'A' class cities, Area I, Area II, and Area III. Major 'A' cities consisted of Bombay, Delhi, Calcutta, Madras and Hyderabad. Area I included areas with a population of 12 lakh and above. Area II included areas with a population of 1 lakh and above with state capitals and capital of union territories not covered in I. Area III consists of areas with a population below one lakh. Officers working in major 'A' cities were provided with a HRA of 25 per cent of basic pay subject to a maximum of Rs. 400. Similarly, officers working in area I, II and III were provided with a HRA of 20 per cent, 15 per cent and 10 per cent respectively with ceiling of Rs. 300 for area I and Rs. 250 for area II and III.

Apart from the general upgrade of the HRA every bipartite, in the sixth bipartite settlement, the ceiling on HRA was removed, which led to a major increase in HRA. After the settlement of the tenth bipartite, officers today are divided into three groups for the provision of the HRA. These divisions are: i) Major 'A' class cities and project area centres in Group A. ii) Other places in Area I, and project area centres in Group B and iii) other places. The officers in these three areas get respectively 9, 8 and 7 per cent of their pay. However, if an officer produces a rent receipt, they will be provided the actual rent paid by them in excess over 0.75 per cent of pay as their HRA. In the eleventh bipartite settlement, the officers' organisations have demanded that the HRA should not increase. This demand came from the fact that sixty per cent of the officers have been staying in leased houses/flats of banks. Thus, the increase in HRA is hardly beneficial to officers.[32]

City Compensatory Allowance (CCA)

City Compensatory Allowance is paid to the officers working in big cities and towns, which included major 'A' class cities and area I. According to the Pillai Committee, the CCA was to be paid at rate of 10 per cent of basic pay subject to a maximum of

Rs. 100 per month. It was payable only so long as an officer is working in the above specified areas.[33] Fifth bipartite settlement, after keeping the above categorisation and increasing the maximum to Rs. 200, introduced another categorisation for CCA. In the new category, an officer working in places with population of 5 lakh and above along with state capitals, Chandigarh, Pondicherry and Port Blair would get 6 per cent of basic pay as CCA with a maximum of Rs. 120 per month.[34] This categorisation remained same till today. For the eleventh bipartite, the officers' organisations have demanded that the classification of centres should change. They have suggested the division of centres into three categories of category I consisting of major metro like Kolkata, Delhi, Mumbai, Chennai, Bangalore among others; category II consisting of metro cities in Area I, which are centres with a population of more than 12 lakhs and state capitals; and category III consisting of centres with a population of one lakh and above and all district headquarters. Further they have demanded that the rate of city compensatory allowance should be 20, 17.5 and 15 per cent of basic pay for the category I, category II and category III respectively. Adding to it, they have demanded that there should not be any ceiling to the city compensatory allowance.[35]

Special Area Allowance

To compensate for working in difficult, inaccessible or expensive places, Pillai Committee recommended that there should be a special area allowance, which would ultimately be at the discretion of bank management. Pillai committee suggested that special area allowance should not exceed Rs. 150 per month for places like Andaman, Nicobar, Laccadive, Minicoy, Mizoram, Arunachal Pradesh, and Ladakh and it should not exceed Rs. 100 per month for all other places. Today, there are different Special Area Allowance for different places.

Project Area Compensatory Allowance

The Project area allowance is paid to employees who are involved in projects and other specific work in an organisation.

It is an amount paid to compensate the expenses incurred in a project by an employee on the behalf of the organisation. According to the Pillai Committee, officers working in project areas should be paid allowances at the rate of Rs. 40 per month in Group A and Rs. 25 per month in Group B areas. Today, after the tenth bipartite, the project area allowance is fixed at Rs. 400 per month for Group A and Rs. 350 per month for Group B areas.

Mid-Academic Year Transfer Allowance

If an officer is transferred from one place to another in the midst of an academic year and they have one or more children studying in school or college in the former place, then a mid-academic year transfer allowance is paid to them. Pillai Committee mandated that one should get Rs. 100 per month from the date of their report to the new place until the end of academic year for all the children. On and from 1 June 2015, the mid academic year transfer allowance has become Rs. 1,100 per month.

Deputation Allowance

Deputation allowances are paid when an officer is deputed to work in a training institution run by the same bank or jointly with other banks or when they are sent on deputation outside his/her parent bank. Pillai committee suggested 10 per cent of the basic pay should be paid in the first case, where as a 20 per cent in the second case. Today, the basis for the payment of deputation allowance has remained the same with deputation allowance of 4 per cent of the basic pay with a maximum of Rs. 2,000 per month in the case of officers deputed in the same bank; and 7.75 per cent of the basic pay with a maximum of Rs. 4,000 per month in the case of an officer deputed outside the bank. For the eleventh bipartite, officers' organisations have said that there is no uniformity in the payment of deputation, therefore they have demanded that deputation allowance should be made uniform all across banking industry.

Officiating Allowance

Pillai Committee recommended that an officer officiating in a higher post for not less than 10 days should be paid an officiating allowance equal to the difference between the basic pay of the higher post and his/her own basic pay, together with a special allowance, if any, attaching to the higher post.

Closing Allowance

Pillai Committee recommended that a closing allowance should be paid to the officers, who do extra work as a result of closing. The closing allowance was fixed at Rs. 150 for each half yearly closing. Later, after the signing of fifth bipartite settlement, it was agreed that officers would be paid a closing allowance if they are posted at a branch where books are closed on 31 March and 30 September. After the settlement of ninth bipartite, the closing allowance was increased to Rs. 250 for each closing. For the eleventh bipartite settlement, the officers' organisations demanded that all officers irrespective of the officer of posting i.e. branch/administrative office should be paid a closing allowance once in every three month, which should be equal to 15 days of their salary.[36]

Split Duty Allowance

If the working days of an officer are split with a minimum interval of two hours, then a split duty allowance of Rs. 25 per month would be paid to them, according to Pillai Committee. After the tenth bipartite, split duty allowance is Rs. 200 per month.

Hill and Fuel Allowance

Hill and Fuel allowances are paid to the officers stationed at higher altitude regions. According to the Pillai Committee, an integrated 'Hill and Fuel' allowance should be paid for officers. For the officers staying at altitudes of and over 1,500 metres, the rate was fixed at 10 per cent of the basic pay subject to a maximum of Rs. 100 per month and 8 per cent of basic pay subject to a maximum of Rs. 75 per month was for officers staying at altitudes of and over 1,000 metres but below 1,500 metre. In the fifth bipartite settlement, another category was added and thus, the places were divided into (a) Places with an altitude of 1000 meters and above but less than 1,500 meters, (b) Places with an altitude of 1500 meters and above but less than 3,000 meters, and (c) Places with an altitude of 3,000 meters and above. After the finalisation of tenth bipartite settlement, the hill and fuel allowances was fixed at 2, 2.5 and 5 per cent respectively of their pay with a maximum of Rs. 750 per month in the first case, Rs. 1,000 per month in the second case and in their case the maximum is fixed at Rs. 200 per month.

Halting allowance

The Pillai Committee also made detailed recommendations for the standardisation of halting and travelling allowance rules relating to journeys performed on duty, on transfer and on retirement. If an officer is transferred to a new place or sent to some other place for the bank's work, she should be paid halting allowances. For the payment of halting allowance, the Pillai Committee again took the division of cities into major 'A' class cities, area I and other place as the criteria. The officers, whose pay range was between Rs. 700 and Rs. 1,200 per month was given Rs. 35, Rs. 30 and Rs. 25 daily for the three cities respectively. Similarly, the officers with the pay scale of Rs. 1,201 per month and above were provided with the halting allowance of Rs. 50, Rs. 40 and Rs. 30 per day for the three cities.

Till the Tenth Bipartite Settlement, the division of cities remained same, with officers in the scale I/II/III getting Rs. 800, Rs. 700 and Rs. 600 respectively in major 'A' class cities, area I and other places and Rs. 1,000, Rs. 800 and Rs. 700 for the officers in scale IV and above. In the Tenth Bipartite Settlement, metros were added as a new category and an improved allowance was attached to all four categories of cities with officers divided into three categories of scales I, II, III, VI and above. The rates are as given in the following chart:

Table 5: Halting Allowance as on 1 June 2015

Grade / Scales of Officers	*Metro (Rs.)*	*Major 'A' Class Cities (Rs.)*	*Area-I (Rs.)*	*Other Places (Rs.)*
Officers in Scale VI & above	1800	1300	1100	950
Officers in Scale IV & above	1500	1300	1100	950
Officers in Scale I / II / III	1300	1100	900	800

Reimbursement of expenses on travel

The Pillai Committee laid down rules for the provision of travel related compensation for an officer, who is required to travel on duty. Different provisions to different grades of officers, which is prevalent even today, were given. With a little change in the provisions laid down by Pillai Committee, the tenth bipartite settlement gave the following provisions:[37]

(a) An officer in the junior management grade is entitled to travel by first class or AC 2-tier sleeper by train. He/She may, however, travel by air (economy class) if so permitted by the competent authority, having regard to the exigencies of business or public interest.

(b) An officer in the middle management grade is entitled to travel by first class or AC 2-tier sleeper by train. He/She may, however, travel by air (economy class) if the distance to be travelled is more than 1,000 kilometres. He may travel by air (economy class) even for a shorter distance if so permitted by the competent authority.

(c) An officer in the senior management or top executive grade is entitled to travel by AC first class by train or by air (economy class).

(d) An officer in the senior management or top executive Grade may travel by car between places not connected by air or rail provided that the distance does not exceed 500 kilometres. However, when a major part of the distance between the two places can be covered by air or rail only the rest of the distance should normally be covered by car.

(e) Any other officer may be authorised by the competent authority, having regard to exigencies of business, to travel by his own vehicle or by taxi or by the bank's vehicle.

Following the above provisions, an officer would be provided the following travel allowance:

I. For air or rail travel, single fare for the officer will be reimbursed.

II. For travel by road by his own vehicle, the cost incurred would be reimbursed depending upon the type of vehicle used and the terrain covered and would be decided by the banks.

III. Whenever hiring a taxi is permitted, the actual charges paid would be reimbursed.

IV. For the travel by public motor or water transport, the actual fare will be reimbursed.

Upon transfer, the cost incurred by an officer for the travel of his/her family members was also made eligible for the reimbursement of first class rail fare.

Apart from the above mentioned travel allowance, an officer is also entitled to leave travel concession facility, which has been recommended to be available for travel to hometown in a block of two years and for travel to any place in India once in a block of 4 years. On retirement, an officer is eligible to claim travelling allowance, baggage and other expenses for themselves and their families as on transfer from the last station at which they were posted to place where they would settle.

Medical Aid

The Pillai Committee also ensured that officers and their families[38] get medical aid facilities. The PCR recommended that an officer should be eligible for reimbursement of medical expenses actually incurred by him in respect of himself and his family. It said that the hospitalisation charges should be reimbursed by the bank to the extent of 75 per cent in the case of an officer and 50 per cent in the case of his family members. Reimbursement of medical expenses was done on the basis of an officer's own certificate of having incurred such expenditure, supported by a statement of accounts for the amount claimed. The ceiling for the reimbursement of medical expenses was fixed at Rs. 500 for officers drawing Rs. 2,001 and more; it was Rs. 300 and Rs. 400 for officers drawing Rs. 700-1,200 per month and Rs. 1,201-2,000 per month respectively.

After the signing of the tenth bipartite settlement, reimbursement ceiling for medical expenses on and after 1 November 2012 was agreed at Rs. 8000 and Rs. 9050 per annum for officers in the junior management grade/middle management grade and the senior management grade and the top executive grade respectively. In the charter of demands for the eleventh bipartite settlement, the officers' organisations have demanded that there should be 100 per cent reimbursement of the medical expenses, for their as well as for the dependent family members.

Transport Allowances

The Pillai Committee made it mandatory for officers to use their private vehicles for official purposes, and recommended that the officers should be compensated for the expenditure at rates fixed by the banks. Besides, the Pillai Committee also suggested that the bank may grant loans for the purchase of a car or any other conveyance. The rules laid out to provide conveyance loan are given in the conveyance loan section.

Loans

Before the implementation of the Pillai Committee, bank officers in different banks were granted different kinds of loans such as loans for floods/droughts, for purchase of consumer goods,

ALL INDIA CONFEDERATION OF
BANK OFFICERS' ORGANISATIONS

STATE BANK OF INDIA SUPERVISING
OFFICIALS ASSOCIATION BOMBAY CIRCLE
REGIONAL CONFERENCE
18-10-1981
WEL-COME

BANK OF INDIA
OFFICIALS ASSOCIATION

STATE
OFFICIALS
REGI

STATE BANK
STATE BANK OF INDIA
SUPERVISING

NO ALLOWANCE
NO ANNUAL CLOSING
WE WANT
GOVT'S INTERVENTION
WE DEMAND
IMMEDIATE
WAGE REVISION
ZINDABAD
STATE BANK OF INDIA
SUPERVISING STAFF ASSOCIATION
(MADRAS CIRCLE)

UNITED FORUM OF BANK UNIONS
CHENNAI
20-09-2002

HISTORIC JOINT INDEFINITE STRIKE
1st ANNIVERSARY
STATE BANK OF INDIA
STATE BANKS
STAFF UNION
CHENNAI CIRCLE

SILVER JUBILEE
AIBOC

ALL INDIA BANK OFFICERS' CONFEDERATION
SPECIAL EXECUTIVE COMMITTEE MEETING
On the eve of

JOINT DHARNA

ALL INDIA BANK OFFICERS' CONFEDERATION
NATIONAL WOMEN'S CONVENTION
4TH & 5TH NOVEMBER, 2017
K.C. COLLEGE, MUMBAI

winter/warm clothing loans, for children or own marriage along with many others at concessional rates. Pillai Committee decided to do away with all these different kinds of loan and only loans that were guaranteed loans for purchase of conveyance and housing.

Conveyance Loan

The Pillai Committee recommended that all the officers were eligible for a loan for the purchase of scooter/motorcycle and the officers drawing basic pay of Rs. 1,200 and above were eligible for the purchase of a car too. For the purchase of scooter/ motorcycle, 90 per cent of the cost was made payable through loan with a maximum of Rs. 4,000, which has to be repaid back within 60 months at an interest rate of 1 per cent less than the sanctioned rate. Similarly, the car loan was provided to bear 80 per cent of the cost with maximum of Rs. 20,000 with same deadline and same reduction in rate.

In the charter of demands for the eleventh bipartite settlement, officers' organisations have said that the conveyance loan has not been revised for long and demanded that the limit of the car loan should be increased to Rs. 15 lakh and for the purchase of two-wheeler loan the limit should be Rs. 1 lakh at a moderate interest and it should be without any slab.[39]

Housing loans

All the confirmed officers with five years of continuous service were made eligible to receive house loan unless they had not received it from any other institutional agency. The Pillai Committee recommended that housing loans should be calculated at the rate of 50 months' basic pay or 80 per cent of the actual cost, whichever is less, subject to a maximum of Rs. 80,000. The loan should be repaid in twenty years at the rate of five per cent. For housing loan too, the officers' organisations in the charter of demands of the eleventh bipartite demanded it to be increased to Rs. 1 Crore.

Leave Facility

The major problem faced by the bank officers during the initial period was with regard to leave facility. Officers did not receive any leave, it is said that it was hard for officers to get leave even for their marriages. That is the reason, the demand for the right over leave became one of the focal point of 1,969 strike in State Bank of India. The Pillai Committee ensured that a minimum amount of leave was guaranteed to officers. It was recommended that officers should be entitled to have privilege, sick, and casual leaves, extraordinary leaves without pay, maternity leave, encashment of leaves, terminal leaves, additional sick leave, and special casual leave.

Casual leave

Casual leave is provided to an officer for 12 working days with full emoluments. However, they cannot avail more than four casual leaves at one time. Today, the officers have demanded that casual leaves should be increased to 15 working days.

Privilege leave

An officer is eligible for privilege leave computed at one day for every 11 days of service, though an officer cannot avail privilege leave before completion of 11 months of their service on duty. On privilege leave too, the officers are entitled to full emoluments for the period of leave. However, a notice must be given a month prior to their intension to avail the leave. In addition, privilege leave could be accumulated more than 180 days. In the tenth bipartite settlement, the officers' unions were able to improve the provisions of privilege leave with 270 days of accumulation and notice period reduced to 15 days. For the eleventh bipartite settlement, they have demanded a privilege leave of 33 days per year, and removal of ceiling on accumulation of leave.

Sick leave

An officer became eligible to avail 30 days sick leave for each completed year of service, which can be added upto 360 days and can be availed at once upon the production of medical certificate by the medical practitioner acceptable to the bank's discretion. An officer is eligible for half the emoluments for the period of leave. It was further added that an officer may avail additional sick leave on completion of 24 years of service. Later, the maximum days of sick leave were increased to 540 days in the fifth bipartite settlement.

Maternity leave

The Pillai Committee provided women officers with a maternity leave of 3 months, which could be availed during pre-natal period or at the time of miscarriage or abortion. However, it should not exceed more than 12 months in the entire period of service as an officer. In 2010, the period of maternity leave was increased to 6 months. In 2015, it was also added that maternity leave may also be provided to a childless female officer for legally adopting a child who is below one year of age for a maximum period of six months. In the same year, paternity leave was also introduced, and a male officer with less than two surviving children became eligible to avail paternity leave of 15 days.

In the charter of demands for the eleventh bipartite settlement, the bank officers have demanded that there should a provision of crèche facility for the children of officers. They have also demanded for a child care leave facility for women officers, as had been provided to central government employees. They have also put forth the demand that the paternity leave should be extended to 60 days for 2 occasions.

Extraordinary leave

Extraordinary leave was made available to officers to avail for 360 days of leave during the entire period of service. Officers availing this leave facility will lose their pay and this leave can't be availed for more than 90 days.

Recall to duty

With the provision of all the above mentioned leaves, the Pillai Committee also made a provision of calling back of the officer from the leave whenever the bank deemed fit. However, if the officer was out of station, the bank was obliged to provide them with the actual expenses incurred by the officer and their family members in their return. Furthermore, if the officer and their family members decide to go back to the same station from which they were called, the expenses of the return journey were also borne by the bank.

Age of Superannuation

Pillai Committee suggested that the age of superannuation of officers in banks should be 60 years, with a provision for review at the age of 58 years to adjudge the fitness of the officer for continuance in service. It was instructed that the review should initiate on the officer attaining the age of 57 years and completed before they reach 58 years. In the latest, charter of demands, the officers' organisations demanded that the age of superannuation should be raised to 65 years for all officers, because there has been a shortage of officers in the middle order due of non-recruitment for 10 years.

Terminal Benefits

Terminal benefits are the final entitlements an officer gets upon the termination of their employment contract. There are a number of monetary benefits that an officer gets on retirement. When an officer retires from the bank service, they are paid a sum equivalent to the emoluments of any period of privilege leave that they have accumulated. Apart from the earned leaves, a system of contributory provident fund and gratuity was recommended by the Pillai Committee.

Provident fund

Provident fund or Employee's Provident Fund is a benefit scheme for officers for their old age after retirement as a compulsory retirement benefit under the Provident Fund Act, 1952. The Pillai Committee recommended a contributory provident fund for all officers unless someone is already a member of the provident fund. In the contributory provident fund, the bank has to contribute to the provident fund of officers according the rule governing this law. However, it should not exceed more than 8.33 per cent of the pay of the officer. For the fifth bipartite settlement, the AIBOC had demanded that the PF contribution should be increased to 10 per cent of the pay, where pay meant basic pay including the DA. The AIBOC could be able to achieve the first part of this demand in the sixth bipartite and the rate of contribution was increased to 10 per cent, however, pay included just the basic pay. In the sixth bipartite settlement, the concept of 'pay' for the purpose of PF was broadened to include stagnation increments, professional qualification allowance and increment component of fixed personal allowance apart from the basic pay. Later, after the seventh bipartite settlement, officiating allowance was also added. In all this while, the IBA never agreed to include dearness allowance for the payment of pf. however, when the officers' organisations along with award staff unions and other unions in financial sector demanded pension as third retirement benefit, the IBA offered DA linked PF to supress this demand and made it clear that pension would be introduced as an alternative to PF. The officers, who were appointed on or before 30 June 1994 were given a choice to choose between pension and DA linked PF. For the employees joining after 1 November 1993, only pension is available.

Gratuity

The Pillai Committee made the provision of gratuity for officers under the Gratuity Act of 1972. According to this act, every officer was eligible for gratuity on retirement, death, disablement rendering him unfit for further service as certified by a medical officer approved by the bank or resignation after completing ten years of continuous service. In the fifth bipartite settlement, it was agreed that the amount of gratuity payable to an officer should be one months' pay for each completed year of service, subject to maximum of 15 months' pay. An officer working for more than 30 years of service was made eligible for additional gratuity for an additional amount at the rate of half of one month's pay. Here 'pay' implies basic pay along with special pay, officiating pay, PQP, and increment component of FPP.

Pension

There was no provision of pension in the Pillai Committee, instead it recommended contributory provident fund and gratuity. However, officers in the SBI were entitled for contributory PF and pension (in lieu of gratuity). Thus, the AIBOC in the charter of demand for the fifth bipartite in 1987 included the demand for pensions as a third benefit in addition to PF and gratuity, but started pressing for it only in the sixth bipartite. In 1989, the RBI unilaterally introduced a pension scheme withdrawing the PF. This was not acceptable to an overwhelming majority of employees of the RBI itself. A similar possibility for the same arose in every bank and other financial institutions. This led the officers, workmen and several employees of other financial institutions to come together. They formed a Joint Action Committee (JAC) in 1990 and pressed for the demand of pension as a third retirement benefit and PF be paid on the basis of basic pay and DA. The JAC met the then Finance Minister Manmohan Singh twice – in 1992 and 1993, a lot of campaigning was undertaken to press for the demand. It has been alleged by the AIBOC, that the AIBEA bought the argument put forth by the IBA that the banks could not afford to pay both pension and PF. Therefore, the AIBEA agreed to the proposal of pension in lieu of PF. However, many other unions did not buy this logic and kept pressing for the demand. In 1993 alone, two strikes were organised – one in March and again in September, and finally a settlement was reached on 29 October 1993. Although pension as a third retirement benefit could not be achieved, the following improvements could be made to post-retirement benefits in the sixth bipartite settlement:

1) PF was reckoned on DA upto Consumer Price Index (CPI) of 1,150 points. 2) Pension would be introduced with effect from 01.11.1993 as an alternative to PF. 3) Exiting employees could opt for DA linked PF or Pension on or before 30.06.1994. 4) for the employees joining after 01.11.1993 there would only be pension and gratuity and no PF. The package was agreed to by all unions and was a product of a prolonged and strong fight by the employees of the financial sector under the banner of the JAC.

The pension scheme agreed to on 29 October 1993 was gazetted in the year 1995 and was called The Bank (Employees') Pension Regulations, 1995. In the eighth bipartite settlement, which started in 2002, pension once again became a major issue as the government sent a communication to all banks instructing that a contributory pension scheme would be introduced for the future recruits in the banks as had been done in the case other government employees. This was opposed by the AIBOC and a memorandum was submitted. The AIBOC also took the matter with the IBA. The officers' organisations, on the other hand, demanded that the payment of pension should be on the basis of the 50 per cent of actual pay drawn; the sharing of cost on account of pension by the employees and officers should continue at 18.25 per cent of basic pay; the IBA should re-consider its stand in regard to the extension of one more option for pension, but the IBA rejected these demands at once. The UFBU met the chairperson of the IBA and put forth their demands. It was assured to them that the issues raised by them would be discussed with the IBA officials as well as the negotiation committee. In the next round of discussion, the IBA said that the demand of pension at 50 per cent of the basic pay would cost an additional Rs. 850 Crores and thus they could not do it. However, in the meeting held on 21 April, they accepted the demand conditioned that the employees and officers would bear 20.25 per cent of the cost. However, the UFBU made it clear that they would not accept any increase beyond 18.25 per cent. Finally, the eighth bipartite was signed on 2 June 2005, where the correction of pension aberration and achievement of 50 per cent of the last drawn pay as pension payable to all employees retired with effect from 1 April 1988 and future retirees.

For the ninth bipartite settlement, one more option to join pension scheme became a major demand from the officers' organisations side.[40] When the pension scheme was introduced, it came with a clause stating that those who would sign up for pension would not have the right to go on 'strike', because of which a large number of officers were prevented from exercising the option. As a result, when the 'strike' clause was withdrawn from the rules, the UFBU demanded that another option should be permitted to the employees in the banking industry. A letter was written by the AIBOC to the IBA in 2006 demanding the IBA to convene a meeting for discussion on the second option in pension. In the meantime, the IBA had circulated a draft proposal to all the members banks advising them to explore the possibility of introducing a new pension scheme. This was done without a discussion with the UFBU, which had strong reservations to the introduction of an alternative scheme in an arbitrary manner. The UFBU urged the IBA to withdraw the scheme. Nonetheless, the IBA made an attempt to introduce the contributory pension scheme in the Bank of India. It was opposed by the UFBU and could not be implemented. Thus, the IBA was forced to come to discuss this issue. On 13 June 2008, a meeting happened between the IBA and the UFBU at Mumbai to decide the cost for the introduction of second option in pension. It decided to form a common panel to study this cost. The common panel submitted its report, which said that the cost of giving pension to those, who have PF would be Rs. 17,000 Crores and if their PF balance (management contribution) is adjusted, then the net deficit was calculated to be Rs. 6,000 Crores. Both side agreed to the data provided by the common panel, but the IBA said that the cost should be shared 50-50 by the officers, whereas the officers' organisations offered 15 per cent of the extra cost. In the next meeting, which happened on 21 January 2009, the IBA increased its share to 60 per cent and asked the officers to pay 40 per cent, while the AIBOC offered to pay 25 per cent, a ten per cent increase from the last time. The meeting that happened on 21 February 2009 gave a new turn to the pension issue as the IBA suggested the introduction of a new pension scheme, i.e., defined contributory scheme. However, this was rejected by the officers' organisations and it was agreed that the IBA would provide a detailed copy of the proposed new pension scheme and only after studying the details any further discussion would take place. It was also agreed that this issue would be kept separate from the existing demand of the second option for pension. However, the new pension scheme was implemented by the IBA for the employees and officers joining the industry on or after 1 April 2010. This generated anger among the officers and they went for protest. Nonetheless, the IBA did not back off from their position and went ahead with the implementation of new pension scheme. However, on 29 June 2010, government cleared the proposal of second option for pension and on 10 August 2010, it was implemented by the IBA. Today, the bank officers are not happy with the new pension scheme, therefore, the officers' organisations have demanded that all the officers should be covered under the old pension scheme, i.e. The Bank (Employees') Pension Regulations, 1995 or ensure an assured Pension.

The discussion above has outlined the intricate details of the struggle for secure and better working conditions that has been led by the AIBOC. Officers in the banking sector are allotted a larger pay compared to award staff at the banks, however the position is disadvantageous within the larger structure of the banking sector. Neither the award staff nor officers has shares in the profits of the bank and both derive their pay from a management that is constantly trying to squeeze them out of their fair share. The fight for equal rights and better conditions is this struggle that emerges from the conflict between the management and the employees. And even though these struggles may seem to be quite small when each of them is considered independently, they together form the great struggle that the bank staff and officers waged for equality and justice.

Notes

1. S.R. Sengupta, *Bank Officers' Movement; Perspective and Journey* (Kolkata: Foundation for United Trade Union Research & Education (FUTURE), 2010), 1.
2. Virenda Kumar, "Committee for Standardization of Pay Scales, Allowances and Perquisites of Officers in the Nationalised Banks, 1973," in *Committees and Commissions in India*, Vol. XI (New Delhi: Concept, 1994), 228.
3. Other Members of Committee were K.P.J. Prabhu, S.M. Joshi and J.M. Lalvani.
4. Virenda Kumar, "Committee for Standardization of Pay Scales, Allowances and Perquisites of Officers in the Nationalised Banks, 1973," in *Committees and Commissions in India*, Vol. XI (New Delhi: Concept, 1994), 229.
5. Ibid., 228.
6. All India Bank Officer' Confederation, *AIBOC – IBA Joint Notes on Wage Revisions* (Bangalore: All India Bank Officer' Confederation, 2010), 24.
7. T. Rosaiah, "Human Resource Management in Commercial Banks" (PhD thesis, Sri Krishnadevaraya University, 1994), 215.
8. Virenda Kumar, "Committee for Standardization of Pay Scales, Allowances and Perquisites of Officers in the Nationalised Banks, 1973," in *Committees and Commissions in India*, Vol. XI (New Delhi: Concept, 1994), 229.
9. This is an exam conducted by Indian Institute of Banking and Finance. The main objective of conducting this exam is to improve the decision-making skills of officers in their particular field and to reward them with additional increment on passing this exam.
10. Virenda Kumar, "Committee for Standardization of Pay Scales, Allowances and Perquisites of Officers in the Nationalised Banks, 1973," in *Committees and Commissions in India*, Vol. XI (New Delhi: Concept, 1994), 229.
11. "State Bank Group - Salary Revision," *Common Bond*, May 1986, 2.
12. Shantha Raju (Former Secretary General of the AICOBOO), interviewed by Sarika Chaudhary, Bangalore, India, February 2018.
13. R.N. Godbole, "Report of the General Secretary to the 1st Session of General Council," *Common Bond*, January 1987, 12.
14. R.N. Godbole, *Revision of Salary Structure of Private Sector Banks Officers* (Bangalore, Karnataka: All India Bank Officers' Confederation (AIBOC), 1985), 1.
15. Ibid.
16. "AIBOC Sphere Widens - Majority Achieved in Private Sector," *Common Bond*, August 1987, 6.
17. All India Bank Officer' Confederation, *AIBOC – IBA Joint Notes on Wage Revisions* (Bangalore: All India Bank Officer' Confederation, 2010).
18. R.N. Godbole, ed., "Salary Revision Finalised," *Common Bond*, October 1985, 1.
19. R.N. Godbole, "Report of the General Secretary to the 1st Session of General Council," *Common Bond*, January 1987, 14.
20. R.N. Godbole, "Report of the General Secretary to the 2nd Session of General Council," *Common Bond*, January 1990, 19.

21. All India Bank Officer' Confederation, *AIBOC – IBA Joint Notes on Wage Revisions* (Bangalore: All India Bank Officer' Confederation, 2010), 3.
22. The formation of UFBU is discussed in the next chapter.
23. Y. Sundershan (Former President of the AIBOC), interviewed by Sarika Chaudhary, Bangalore, India, June 2018.
24. D.S. Rishabadas, *UFBU Circular No. 5 Dated 22 February, 2013,* Circular No. 11 (Bangalore, Karnataka: All India Bank Officers' Confederation (AIBOC), 2013).
25. Ibid.
26. D.S. Rishabadas, *10th Bipartite Meeting Scheduled for 4 March, 2013; Postponed,* Circular No. 12 (Bangalore, Karnataka: All India Bank Officers' Confederation (AIBOC), 2013).
27. D.S. Rishabadas, *10th Bipartite – Road Blocks in the Negotiations the AIBOC Is Fully Prepared to Overcome,* Circular No. 21 (Bangalore, Karnataka: All India Bank Officers' Confederation (AIBOC), 2013).
28. Y. Sundershan (Former President of the AIBOC), interviewed by Sarika Chaudhary, Bangalore, India, June 2018.
29. Ibid.
30. Ibid.
31. AIBOC et al., *Charter of Demands Submitted to IBA on 2 May 2017,* PDF, March 29, 2018, 30.
32. AIBOC et al., *Charter of Demands Submitted to IBA on 2 May 2017,* PDF, March 29, 2018, 30.
33. Virenda Kumar, "Committee for Standardization of Pay Scales, Allowances and Perquisites of Officers in the Nationalised Banks, 1973," in *Committees and Commissions in India,* Vol. XI (New Delhi: Concept, 1994), 230.
34. All India Bank Officer' Confederation, *AIBOC – IBA Joint Notes on Wage Revisions* (Bangalore: All India Bank Officer' Confederation, 2010), 40.
35. AIBOC et al., *Charter of Demands Submitted to IBA on 2 May 2017,* PDF, March 29, 2018, 32.
36. AIBOC et al., *Charter of Demands Submitted to IBA on 2 May 2017,* PDF, March 29, 2018, 37.
37. Harvinder Singh, *A Long Drawn Battle Concludes – 10th Bipartite Settlement Signed,* Circular No. 25 (Bangalore, Karnataka: All India Bank Officers' Confederation (AIBOC), 2015), 13.
38. Pillai Committee defined family for this purpose as consisting of spouse, wholly dependent children and wholly dependent parents.
39. AIBOC et al., *Charter of Demands Submitted to IBA on 2 May 2017,* PDF, March 29, 2018, 71.
40. G.D. Nadaf (Former General Secretary of the AIBOC), interviewed by Sarika Chaudhary, Bangalore, India, February 2018.

4
Milestones and the Ongoing Struggles

In the course of its 33 years of existence, the AIBOC has been at the forefront of many struggles. In the previous chapters, we have seen how the AIBOC raised the question of equal pay for equal work and got the officers of the banks across India their due share in wages. Although bipartite negotiations are one of most important method of collective bargaining for the officers in the banking sector; however, it is not the only one. In addition, there are innumerable number problems faced by the officers that were not a part of the bipartite negotiations like discriminations and victimisations faced by officers. Further, the AIBOC has also expanded its reach beyond the banking sector to other financial institutions. Therefore, in the fight for better working conditions of the officers in the banking and financial sector, the AIBOC has also taken up other methods of collective bargaining like direct confrontations with the managements or even the governments, lobbying, reaching out to the larger public and even approaching the courts.

Apart from the struggles for the better working conditions for the officers, the AIBOC has also taken up the issues concerning banking sector, in particular and society in general. It was a major force in opposing the liberalisation policies adopted by the government in 1991. In this section, we shall look at the different struggles that the AIBOC led and was a part of, whether they be for better working conditions, or for an equal treatment and the ideals of social banking. These struggles constitute the milestones of the AIBOC's history.

The First Challenge and the AIBOC's Response

Immediately after its formation, the first challenge before the AIBOC was the issue of premature retirement.[1] A serious point of conflict arose in between the government and bank officers. After nationalisation, the banks had played an important role in implementing government policies. One such scheme formulated in 1983 was 'loan melas', under which mass loaning programme were launched by the nationalised banks. It was directed that people belonging to the lower sections of society should be given loans and the discretion of identification of borrowers was vested with the branch managers. There were many instances of false loan sanctioning. It was also found that fake application forms were being sold in the open market. In this direction, the West Bengal unit of the AIBOC submitted a memorandum to the Bankers' Committee drawing their attention to this; however, no steps were taken to remedy this.[2] Instead, bank officers were accused that they were sanctioning fictitious loans. Therefore, directions were given to the banks that inefficient officers should be suspended through the powers granted to the management under the regulation of 19(1) and 20(1). The Bank of Baroda retired 16 officers in this manner. There was a possibility of retirement in other banks as well. Word was going round that the government had set targets for each bank and that the targeted retirements were to be made effective before 31 December. Repeated statements were made by the Minister of State for Finance Janardhan Poojary regarding the removal of corrupt and inefficient officers in the banks. All this added to the scare in the banking industry and it was feared that any officer could be forced to retire. In the wake of this development, an urgent Executive Committee meeting was held at New Delhi on 19 and 20 December 1985, where it was decided that a collective action was necessary to meet the threat from the government and the managements. Accordingly, a programme of action was drawn up, which included demonstrations by the affiliates before their respective head officers, protest telegrams to be sent to the Prime Minister. The copies of this letter were also sent to the Finance Minister,

Chairman of IBA and to the AIBOC central office combined demonstration by all affiliates at all state capitals and a dharna before the banking department of the Ministry of Finance on 24 January 1986.[3] The organisation took up the task with all seriousness, and an agitation was launched throughout the country.

In the wake of the agitation by the AIBOC, the IBA and the government reacted and came out with a press statement saying that there was no intention to prematurely retire officers on a large scale.[4] A meeting was also held between the government and the officers' organisations on 28 January 1986. Because of the changed attitude of the government and the IBA, the AIBOC postponed the dharna planned on 24 January and instead a demonstration was held in front of the State Bank of India, local head office in Parliament Street.[5] Through its agitations, the AIBOC was able to stop the victimisation of officers through the tool of premature retirement and earlier government directions to the banks on a wide-scale premature retirement were stayed immediately.

There were many instances of victimisation, which came up during the initial days of the AIBOC.The issue of premature retirement was still to be settled, when three officers of the Indian Bank were terminated by the management in 1986.[6] It was done under the regulation 20(1) of Bank Officers' Service Regulations, which gave the management power to terminate the services of its employees without holding an enquiry. It was accused by the AIBOC that this was done to victimise officers as they refused to clear applications for 'loan melas'. This was just one of the many instances when this regulation was used by the management to victimise officers. Against this regulation, many court cases were filed by the different constituents of the AIBOC. In the case of Amarjit Singh of Punjab National Bank, Delhi High Court held that his removal from service was illegal and awarded compensation. Bombay High Court in Oriental Bank of Commerce case and Patna High Court in Central Bank's case had said that regulation 20(1) of Bank Officers' Service Regulations offends Article 14 and 16 of right to equality of the Constitution and had declared the regulation as invalid. Thereafter an amendment was made to the service regulation.

Representatives on the Board of Banks

Another challenge before the AIBOC was in the form of the government circular dated 23 August 1982, which directed the bank managements to get away with the old norm of appointing officers' representatives and employees' representatives belonging to the majority union. Under the Banking Companies (Acquisition and Transfer of Undertakings) Act 1970, the employees of the banks were given the choice to select their representatives on the Board of the Banks. However, this right came to the bank employee only in late 1970s, when incorporation of members belonging to majority unions into the boards of banks were done. However, the 1982 circular suggested that the appointment should be done based on performance and ability. The AIBOC alleged that the circular was to give appointments to the officers belonging to the INTUC, which was the trade union front of the Congress. Against this circular, a writ petition was filed by the AIBOC in the Supreme Court. The judgement struck down this circular and ordered that the old norm should be followed in appointing officers in the board of banks. This was a major victory for the AIBOC and its affiliates, which represented an overwhelming majority of officers in 21 banks and in many other banks where it was the largest organisation.[7]

Leading the Struggles for Dignity

The premature retirement was not the only method for the bank managements to harass bank employees. There were many instances, when bank officers were suspended and transferred unilaterally. One such instance was the victimisation of officers of the UCO Bank. It was a time when the banking sector was growing; however, there were hardly any new recruitment. This led to an increase in the workload per officer. Due the lack of supervision, frauds and irregularities were growing and officers were held accountable for these frauds and suspended without any investigation. Moreover, the suspension used to continue for indefinite periods. This attitude of management led to a tremendous amount of dissatisfaction and anger among the officers. Despite efforts by the All India UCO Bank Officers' Federation, no heed was paid to the demands of the officers. Thus, the federation decided to commence agitation from 12 July 1988, which led to unrest in banks.[8]

It was not the case of one bank, industrial relations were very poor in most banks and conflicts were quite common. Between the periods of 1986 and 1989, apart from the UCO Bank, there were serious conflicts that arose in the Central Bank, the Punjab National Bank, the Corporation Bank, the Indian Overseas Bank, the New Bank of India and Dena Bank. Amongst the private sector banks, where serious industrial relations conflicts ensued were the Lakshmi Vilas Bank, the Bank of Madura, the Federal Bank, the Dhanalakshmi Bank and the South Indian Bank. The AIBOC intervened positively in all these industrial disputes and extended its support to affiliates in their respective banks. In many cases, it was able to resolve the dispute. Further, it demanded that all managements should recognise the existence of the officers' unions and decisions should be taken in consultation with the unions.[9]

Another major issue that came up in front of the AIBOC and other unions was the problem of the wage freeze in UCO Bank. In response to this victimisation, an unprecedented solidarity was forged amongst the unions. On 4 February 1997, the AIBOC along with other officers' and employees unions organized a rally in Calcutta condemning the role of government nominee on the board of the UCO Bank. It was a massive show of strength, which forced the government to instruct the management of the UCO Bank to place the matter in the board for reconsideration. 20 February 1997 became a day of celebration as the decision of wage freeze was taken back.

However, this victory was not momentary, rather it was to last forever as this struggle led to the formation of the United Forum of Bank Unions (UFBU). During this struggles all the nine unions in the financial sector – AIBEA, the AIBOC, NCBE, AIBOA, BEFI, INBOC, INBEF, NOBO and NOBW – representing almost 100 per cent of workmen and officers came together to form the UFBU.[10] Even after the victory in the issue of wage freeze in the UCO Bank, the UFBU continued to function on the basis of a common minimum programme, which included (a) resistance to the establishment of local area private banks; (b) non-implementation of the pension agreement in private banks and the removal of the strike clause in pension regulation; (c) non-implementation of the 6 Bipartite Settlements in the RRBs; (d) removal of the ban on recruitment and compassionate appointments and (e) removal of the ceiling on gratuity and bonus. The UFBU, thereafter, had played a vital role as a representative of bank employees. It has been at the forefront of wage negotiations and other struggles.[11] Thus, the formation of UFBU was a major event in the history of bank officers' movement.

AIBOC and the Fight Against the Privatisation of Banks

The biggest challenge that presented itself to the AIBOC was the threat of privatisation of public sector banks. After the Government of India adopted the policy of liberalisation, privatisation and globalisation in 1991, the banking industry was in the eye of the storm of the new fiscal and industrial policies of the government. A serious threat of denationalisation of banks was posed by the government in July 1991, and this led to a widespread protest by the employees and officers in the banking industry. A Joint Action Committee of bank unions comprising of the AIBEA, the AIBOC, the NCBE, the BEFI and the AIBOA was formed on 2 August 1991, when the representatives of the mentioned organisations met at Calcutta for the purpose to consider the situation arising out of the proposed denationalisation of banks by the government. The committee concluded with a unanimous decision to oppose this move and gave a call for the first nationwide strike on 6 September 1991.[12] The AIBOC coordinated with the central trade unions to oppose the proposed economic reforms. A meeting of central trade unions and the national federation was held at New Delhi on 13 August 1991, where it was decided to oppose the recent economic policies announcement by the Government of India. The meeting decided to hold an All India Convention against the economic policies of the Government of India on 16 September 1991 to prepare a programme of action culminating in one day all india strike in industrial undertakings.[13] The strike called by the Joint Action Committee (JAC) on 6 September was averted when the government gave an assurance on the floor of the Parliament that banks would not be denationalised.[14] However, that did not ensure the officers' organisation that the threat of privatisation was gone as one of the conditions for the IMF loan was the 'privatisation of banks', therefore the Joint Action Committee decided to remain intact with the AIBOC, the AIBEA, the BEFI and the AIBOA as its members. They met on 16 September 1991, where they deliberated on further steps to maintain organisational pressure to forestall any move on the part of the government. They then decided to organise national and state level conventions[15] leading to an all India strike on 29 November 1991. The strike was successful with all the banks, insurance companies and many factories were closed, but despite this, the government did not enter into a negotiation with the trade unions. A national convention of public sector officers was also held on 9 and 10 March 1992 at Delhi, which denounced the new economic policies of the government.

During that period, the Ministry of Finance commissioned a committee to study India's financial system. The committee was headed by M. Narasimham, a former Governor of the RBI. The AIBOC submitted a memorandum to the committee, urging that all state sector banks be merged to form a National Banking Corporation of India and that the NBC may set up subsidiaries on functional or geographical basis.[16] The Narasimham Committee submitted its report to the government on 20 November 1991. The report observed that that there was a decline in the productivity and efficiency of the state owned banks, and suggested some changes in their operational structure. The Committee suggested a division of banking system into four categories. The first category included four large banks (principally the State Bank of India), which was supposed to compete internationally. The second category was the national banks numbering up to ten, which were meant to engage in universal banking. The last two tiers of the banking system were proposed to be local and rural banks. The local banks were supposed to look after banking in specific regions, while rural banks would be engaged in financing agriculture and other related industries. One of the most controversial recommendations was the restructuring of state-owned banks through the process of mergers and acquisition. Though the committee also included the provision that state-owned banks should be 'market-driven',[17] however it did not suggest any concrete step towards it. In addition, the committee suggested that there should not be any further nationalisation of private banks and recommended the abolition of branch licensing. The AIBOC opposed the recommendations of the Narasimham Committee and organised workshops and seminars to educate its members against its ill effects.[18] On 30 October 1992, it instructed all its affiliates and state units to send protest messages to the Government of India against the Narasimham Committee Recommendations.[19] In the third General Council, the AIBOC passed a resolution rejecting the recommendations of the Narasimham Committee (Annexure 6).

Meanwhile, the AIBOC also launched a central trade union for officers, called the Professional Workers' Trade Union Centre of India (PWTUC), which came into existence on 9 March 1992.[20] Through this platform, they envisioned to take the issue of bank officers to the larger public.[21] The founding conference of the PWTUC was held on 4 June 1992 at Delhi. Another strike was called by the officers' organisations with the PWTUC also being a part of it on 16 June 1992 against the New Economic Policies. In addition, the third General Council passed a resolution (Annexure 7) opposing the structural adjustment policy taken up by the government as it undermined the economic sovereignty of India.

There was an all-out campaign made by the government and others who were in the favour of privatisation, that the cause of all economic problems was the public sector. The notion was being created that once these institutions were privatised, the nation's economic woes would be laid to rest. Therefore, there was an amendment made to the Banking Companies (Acquisition & Transfer of Undertakings) Acts 1970/1980 enabling the banks to raise capital by public issue of shares, so that the central government would hold not less than 51 per cent of the share of the nationalised banks. In this direction, the equity held by the government in public sector banks were encashed in three instalments, to mobilise resources to bridge the budgetary gap.

All this led to added responsibility on the unions in the banking sector to defend the existence and need for the public sector banks. The JAC was actively protesting throughout the country to counter this narrative. They organised workshops, seminars and used trade union platforms to put forth their position. Even the officers were instructed to give all their efforts to counter the idea posed by the government that the majority of the banks were sick and they should be privatised. The efforts by officers, award staffs and their unions proved fruitful, when at the end of the financial year, i.e. 31 March 1992, the data showed that except for UCO Bank, Punjab and Sind Bank and the New Bank of India, all other public sector banks showed better working results. The net profits in almost all the banks in the financial year 1994-95 had increased. Thus, the panic which was sought to be created during the last three years about the possibility of some of the banks closing down was rendered unsuccessful.

Bank officers were at the forefront of the struggle against the economic policies of government. The banking industry was on a total shut down on 29 November 1991 and 16 June 1992, when bank officers went on a strike. This attracted the attention of the government. The Finance Minister in a meeting with the chief executives of the Banks asked the banks the reason for even the senior officers to join the strike. The Government of

India later directed the banks to advise officers of scale IV and above that they should not join strikes called by associations of officers belonging to scale I to III. This move of government was out rightly opposed by the officers' organisations.

These efforts of trade unions in conjunction with the left parties were able to delay the process of privatisation but once India became a signatory to the World Trade Organisation (WTO), it was required of them to comply with its provisions and directives. In the financial sector, three international agreements were concluded in February, March and December 1997 on basic communication, information technology and financial services respectively. The AIBOC opposed such agreements on the basis that the so-called equal treatment in the world market would not be possible as the parties were unequal here. They were afraid that while the foreign banks and insurance companies would enter the markers of emerging economies, the reverse would not be possible. In the backdrop of the agreed settlements, India was required to make suitable changes. Thus, the Tarapore Committee was appointed to look at capital account convertibility, Narasimham Committee II for the second phase of reforms in the financial sector, S.H. Khan Committee and R.V. Gupta Committee were also appointed to look at functioning banks.

The Tarapore Committee for Capital Account Convertibility (CAC) was constituted by the Reserve Bank of India. It submitted its report in May 1997 suggesting a roadmap on the full convertibility of rupee on capital account. It covered the capital account convertibility for three years (1997-2000). Another committee which was commission by the RBI to review India's banking system was the Khan Committee. It was headed by S.H. Khan, who was the chairman of the Industrial Development Bank of India (IDBI). The Khan report attempted to harmonise the organisational structure with the lending functions of state-owned commercial banks and development finance institutions.[22]

The Narasimham Committee II was appointed by the government, which submitted its report in April 1998. The report was a reform package for public sector banks. Besides seeking to reduce the government stake to 33 per cent, the committee suggested a massive restructuring programme with full liberty to market forces to determine the process by amalgamations, mergers and closures. Narasimham Committee II recommendations on human resource development and working environment included a reduction in staff, remuneration for employees to be fixed through negotiations at the bank level and for officers to be decided by market forces, and suggested fast automation and mechanisation to match present competition. Another controversial point of the Narasimham Committee II was the division of banks into 'strong' and 'weak' banks. It defined a weak bank as 'it should be one whose accumulated losses and net Non-performing assets (NPAs) exceed its net worth or one whose operating profits less its income on recapitalisation bonds is negative for three consecutive years.' There were also suggestions that 'weak' banks should be closed down. The AIBOC took this position that all these committees were efforts to 'destroy public sector ownership of banks, to replace developmental banking with a profit oriented approach, and eliminate social lending to create a sense of insecurity in the minds of officers and employees all in the name of global competition'.[23]

Apart from the wage negotiation, the UFBU also played an important role in waging a united struggle against the privatisation of nationalised banks. When the Narasimham Committee II was appointed, UFBU appeared before it on 10 March 1998 and presented its view opposing the first Narasimham Committee Recommendations and suggestions for the better functioning of public sector banks.[24] However, when the committee gave its recommendations, none of the suggestions of the UFBU, was included instead opposition was the case. Therefore, the UFBU in its meeting held at Delhi on 27 and 28 April 1998 decided to reject the recommendations. They wrote a memorandum to the Government of India stating their position vis-a-vis the Narasimham Committee.[25] In this way, the UFBU became a united force for all the working people in the banks. In the fifth General Council meeting, the AIBOC celebrated the formation of UFBU.[26]

The fifth General Council meeting also took the issue of performance in the banking sector seriously. Before the General Council, a study group was made to study the performance of the banking sector as there were notions being built that banks were not performing well and they should be privatised. The report of the study group was circulated in the General Council. The report also informed about the impact of shifting approaches from social banking to profit banking on the performance of the banking industry. The report also found that all policies, rules, and guidelines that were adopted as a consequence of the new economic policy along with redefining of the small scale industry, addition to lists of priority sector advances, not-so-strict monitoring of compliance with social lending schemes have led to the huge problem of NPAs. They even alleged that the government for not making any efforts to educate and compel the borrowers to repay their dues to the banks within schedule. The report observed that the total NPAs at that time were around Rs. 45,000 Crores, which comprised of NPAs to big industrial houses and their allies to well over Rs. 37,000 Crores leaving the rest to small agricultural, small industrial and social lending. The report further said that if the Rs. 37,000 Crores were recovered, which they thought was recoverable, Indian banking would be far better. However, for that the need for legal reform, they thought, was extremely important. They suggested that laws should be so amended that the wilful defaulters are brought under criminal proceedings and special courts should be set up to proceed with the cases. Professional properties of promoters and directors should be attached immediately. They also demanded that the secrecy clause should be amended enabling the publication of defaulters' list in the leading dailies and the wilful defaulters should be disqualified from any electoral office. The report concluded by saying that there would be no weak banks if the policies would be directed to recover NPAs.[27]

The General Council, further discussed the specific problems faced by the UCO Bank, the UBI and the Indian Bank as they were the ones termed as 'weak' and there were talks to close them down. The AIBOC had a discussion with the affiliates in these three banks and came with a detailed action plan to be submitted to the RBI and the government. In the study report called 'public sector bank sought to be termed as weak', the AIBOC found the problem behind the poor performance of a few banks is the non-recovery of larger sum of money borrowed by the large and medium industrial houses.[28] Apart from suggesting methods to recover those NPAs, the report also suggested that government should divert their good accounts from so called strong banks to these banks as a short term measure. They also demanded that the government should give capital support till the banks come back to the roads of profit.[29] The report on weak banks was submitted to parliamentarians seeking their intervention. The efforts of the AIBOC in mobilising opinion for the efforts to revive banks were successful when the government decided to release Rs. 400 Crores capital to the UCO Bank, the UBI, and the Indian Bank.[30]

The short term problems of closing down of banks were diverted but the problem still existed. Therefore, the government appointed a seven member Working Group for Revival of Public Sector Banks under the chairpersonship of M.S. Verma, the former chairman of SBI.[31] The terms of reference of the working group were (a) criteria for identification of weak public sector banks; (b) to study and examine the problems of weak public sector banks; (c) to undertake a case by case examination of weak public sector banks and to identify those which are potentially revivable; and (d) to suggest a strategic plan of financial, organisational and operational restrictions for weak public sector banks.[32] Since, the fate of not just these three banks but the whole banking sector depended on the report of this committee, the issue was taken up seriously by all bank unions. The UFBU decided to meet the bank unions in the UBI, the UCO Bank and the Indian Bank to formulate its viewpoint on the issue of 'weak' banks and submit a united memorandum to the M.S. Verma Committee.

On 20 May 1999, UFBU met the Verma Committee and presented their view on the issue of the 'health of banking industry' with a special reference to three 'weak' banks and a memorandum was submitted (Annexure 8). In reply, the M.S. Verma said that the committee was already studying the health of entire financial sector with the aim of finding a solution for everyone. The UFBU made it clear that they stood for the improvement of the public sector banks but any attempt of singling out the employees and officers would be resisted.[33]

The Verma Committee report was published on 4 October 1999. The recommendations of the committee came as a shock to the banking unions. The committee did not even consider NPAs as a cause behind the poor performance of banks and instead it classified the banks on the basis of efficiency parameters. These parameters included (a) capital adequacy ratio (b) coverage ratio (c) return on assets (d) net interest margin (e) ratio of operating profit to average working funds (f) ratio of cost to income and (g) ratio of staff cost to net interest income plus all other incomes.[34] On the basis of these seven efficiency bars, the Indian Bank, the UCO Bank and the United Bank of India were declared as weak banks. Only two banks, the Oriental Bank of Commerce and the State Bank of Patiala were able to meet all seven efficiency parameters. On the basis of this classification the Verma Committee proposed that poorly performing and overstaffed public sector banks should adopt a voluntary retirement scheme that would affect 25 per cent of the staff.[35]

As none of the suggestions of the UFBU were taken into consideration and unilateral recommendations were given, the UFBU called for a meeting on 12 October 1999 to decide the steps to be taken in tackling the problems related to the Verma Committee Report.[36] The unions present there unanimously rejected the report. After detailed discussions, they questioned the efficiency parameter selected by the committee and asserted that social banking was a major reason for the nationalisation of banks, which was not even considered by the committee. They, therefore, decided that the UFBU would launch an agitation with a view to popularise the real causes for the illness of the banking industry, which were the NPAs. They decided to make public the measures suggested by them, that is the publication of list of defaulters of over Rs. 10 lakhs, declare defaulters in bank loans as criminal, setting up of special courts for speedy recovery of bank loans, and bringing to those in the political and bureaucratic level responsible for the creation of huge NPAs. It was further decided that the UFBU would take up the following programmes culminating into a one day strike in the last week of November 1999: Demonstration before bank branches on 27 October 1999 and demonstration before the head offices of banks on 29 October 1999; seminars in State capitals by the second week of November 1999; delegations to the central trade unions and the Members of Parliament seeking their support in the struggles by first week of November; a delegation and memorandum to the Finance Minister, Governor, Reserve Bank of India and all concerned; strike by the end of November 1999.

The programme of action taken up by UFBU was followed up by all its affiliates and on 11 October demonstrations were held before the office of RBI in all state capitals. A delegation of UFBU also met Bimal Jalan, the Governor of the Reserve Bank of India on 9 November 1999 and urged him to reject the report and requested to initiate positive and concrete steps to revamp the so-called weak banks.[37] UFBU also reiterated its position of huge NPAs as the cause for the poor performance of banks and suggested the steps that should be taken to counter it.

The crisis in the banking sector was still on when the government came up with the Insurance Regulatory Development Authority (IRDA) Bill, 1999.[38] The bill proposed to open up the Insurance Sector to the private companies. This bill was opposed by the unions in banking and finance sector on the grounds that opening up the insurance sector would harm the working of public sector insurance companies, which they asserted to have successfully fulfilled their dual duty of providing insurance and resource development. A joint meeting of trade unions from banks and insurance sectors was held in Mumbai on 10 November, where they decided to go for a joint plan of action to counter the privatisation of banking and insurance sector. The meeting decided a march to the parliament on 29 November 1999 against the IRDA bill.[39] However, they were unsuccessful in making it a big campaign, only a march to the LIC building was held at Pondicherry on the decided date. Finally, the IRDA bill was passed by the parliament on 4 December 1999.[40] Nevertheless, the struggle against the privatisation of banks continued.

The 37th Executive Committee meeting of the AIBOC, which was held at Calcutta on 9 and 10 of March 2000 discussed all the issues faced by the banking sector like the issue of privatisation of banks, recovery of the NPAs and the restructuring of weak banks. The meeting countered the claim made by the government that even after the proposed disinvestment of equity from 51 per cent to 33 per cent the banks would be maintained by the government. They claimed that it was nothing but 'misleading'. They also criticised the government for not doing much in regard to the recovery of NPAs. They said that apart from increasing the number of Debt Recovery Tribunals (DRTs), no specific legal action had been taken to recover NPAs. They also opposed the idea to implement the Verma Committee Recommendations of downsizing the workforce, the adaption of Voluntary Retirement Scheme (VRS) and wage freeze as cost saving measures. Therefore, the Executive Committee took up a countrywide 'Save Banks Campaign' from 3 April to 19 April to take the matter to the larger public.[41] The following programmes were taken up by the AIBOC: Demonstrations in front of the head office/zonal office/regional offices of banks on 3 April 2000; district/ state level conventions between 3 and 15 April 2000; telegrams to the Prime Minister and the Union Finance Minister by affiliates/district/state units between 17 and 19 April 2000 and memorandums to different levels of government and political representatives.

While the campaign was going on, another issue of wage freeze in the UCO Bank, the Indian Bank and the United Bank of India came to the fore. The AIBOC along with other organisations under the banner of the UFBU served a notice to the IBA demanding the implementation of the agreement on salary revision signed on 14 December 1999 in three banks as soon as possible. They decided to go for an all India strike on 26 April 2000. Since in a meeting the IBA assured that they stand by the agreement and will ensure its implementation, the strike was deferred. After this meeting, the IBA advised the banks to release the payment to the bank employees in the three banks and also directed to release the arrears. This was a victory to the bank unions, but this was not the only victory. The UCO Bank and the UBI were able to revive itself and it was huge moral victory against those who were suggesting the closing down of these banks.[42] The UCO Bank had witnessed a complete turnaround in 1999-2000 over the previous year from net loss of Rs. 68 Crores in 1998-99 to a net profit of Rs. 36.64 Crores. This was a considerable improvement in the bank's business with deposits growing by 14.34 per cent and advances by 19 per cent. It was also able to reduce its net non-performing assets (NPAs) ratio to net advances from 10.83 per cent in 1998-99 to 8.75 per cent in 1999-2000. This performance of the UCO Bank was comparable with most other banks. Similarly, the United Bank of India was able to manage net profit for three consecutive years and was also able to bring down its net NPA level from 14.7 to 12.7 per cent in 1999-2000. These two banks were the banks with the highest levels of NPA recovery. Business per employee increased by 16 per cent from Rs. 86 lakh to Rs. 100 lakh in the same period.[43]

All this while, the UFBU continued its struggle against the threat of privatisation and took action-oriented programmes like strike, memorandums to ministers and general awareness and opinion mobilisation programmes. The threat of privatisation became an actuality when the privatisation bill titled 'Banking Companies (Acquisition and Transfer of Undertakings) and Financial Institutions Laws (Amendment) Bill, 2000' was introduced in the parliament on 13 December 2000.[44] Because of the campaigns taken up by the AIBOC, the UFBU and other unions the introduction of bill was not easy for the government. The opposition parties forced a division on the floor for the introduction of the bill, those who were supporting the bill were 209 while opposing were 159.[45] While introducing the bill, the Union Finance Minister reiterated the explanation that the amendment would not lead to the disinvestment of government equity.

United Forum of Bank Unions (UFBU) denounced the privatisation bill and an emergency meeting at Calcutta on 14 December 2000 was held, where the plan of action was decided. On the instruction of the UFBU, all affiliates organised protest rallies in all metropolitan centres and in state capitals, which culminated into a nationwide strike on 21 December 2000.[46] The UFBU thanked the opposition parties for coming forward in defence of the nationalised banks and calling the introduced bill 'anti-people'. The Parliament march organised by the UFBU on 28 November, many MPs came forward to support the protest.[47] The campaigns and struggles by the bank employees under the banner of the UFBU was successfully able to stop the Banking Companies (Acquisition and Transfer of Undertakings) and Financial Institutions Laws (Amendment) Bill, 2000. However, the threat of privatisation is never gone. Immediately after this, on 9 May 2001, the Union Cabinet decided to remove all limits on foreign direct investments (FDI) in key sectors. In the banking sector, the decision was to raise the foreign equity to 49 per cent from 20 per cent. This decision was opposed by the AIBOC. The AIBOC along with other unions in the banking sector were able to delay the process, but finally on 5 March 2004 the government announced an increase in the cap on foreign equity in private sector banks to 74 per cent, however they could not increase FDI in public sector banks. Through the constant efforts of the AIBOC along with the UFBU, the privatisation of public sector banks could be resisted.

AIBOC and the Fight for Ideal Social Banking

The nationalised banks play an important part in implementing the policies of the government and thus, in the developmental process. However, despite the extra work done by the bank employees to implement government policies, their efforts are hardly recognised. Many a times, the intensity of conflict increases as we have seen in the case of 'Loan Melas'. In recent times, the implementation of demonetisation was one such incident. On the night of 8 November 2016, on the announcement of Prime Minister Narendra Modi, the currency notes of Rs. 500 and Rs. 1000 were demonetised. The primary purpose of this initiative was purported to tackle 'black money'. However, the scheme failed terribly in tackling this problem;[48] however, it created immense working pressure on the bank employees. Initially, bank unions also thought that this scheme was for the betterment of the nation; therefore, they did not ask for extra remuneration and worked for extra hours. However, later on employees were charged penalties for processing fake notes. This has led to resentment among the bank employees with a firm demand that the timing of the banks should be regulated. The AIBOC also came up with a booklet called *The Critical Analysis of Demonetisation* written by D Thomas Franco, the present General Secretary of the AIBOC. The booklet suggested the ill effects of demonetisation on Indian economy. Addressing a seminar on the same issue at the constitution club in Delhi, D Thomas Franco also demanded that the RBI Governor should take the responsibility and should resign from his post. In addition, the RBI through a notification asked the bank officers' to seek reasons from the customers for late deposits. Bank officers refused this instruction and in reply declared that it was not their duty to police customers. Under the leadership of the then General Secretary Harvinder Singh, a protest demo was held on 21 December 2016 in front of the RBI headquarters at Delhi.[49] The protesting officers were detained for some time in the Parliament Street police station, where the officers continued their protest inside the station.[50] Thus, the AIBOC was at the forefront in criticising this scheme.

After one year of demonetisation, the AIBOC also organised a seminar at Jawaharlal Nehru University, where they came out with detailed data of 158 cases of hoarding new currency. However, nothing was done by the government in this regard. They further demanded that the government should come out with the report on the net result of demonetisation.

As we discussed in this chapter, public sector banks were faced with the constant threat of privatisation after the adaptation of liberalisation policies in 1991. Although there is no denying that the banking industry today is faced with many problems like the huge burden of non-performing assets, incurring significant losses and a low credit growth,[51] however, the solution does not lie in the privatisation of nationalised banks. So, believes the All India Bank Officers' Confederation. To counter the narrative that all the problems faced by the banks would be solved once privatised, the AIBOC set up an Independent Commission on Banking and Financial Policy under the chairmanship of S.P. Shukla, former Secretary of Finance.[52] The Committee consisted of renowned economists like Prabhat Patnaik, C.P. Chandrashekar, Amiya Kumar Bagchi, S.L. Shetty and Sukanya Ghosh. The Committee was requested to come out with its report by the middle of March 2005 to be presented to the government for consideration. The commission at its meeting held at Delhi on 15 March 2005 finalised its interim report. A press meet was held on 15 afternoon to release the summary conclusion of the commission on various issues dealt by it. The commission members along with the AIBOC's leaders addressed the press and explained the objective of the commission was to defend the public sector character of banks.[53] The press was also given an exhaustive picture as to how over the last 15 years, the banking industry was drifting from its objective of social banking to mere profit making. This report has proven very useful to the organisation in countering the constant threat of privatisation.

The AIBOC has made constant endeavours to keep the banking policy in India towards social banking. For this, the AIBOC has worked as watchdog on the policies of the government. Whenever a policy is announced, the AIBOC put its perspective towards that policy. Apart from regularly publishing papers, organising seminars and writing to the concerned authorities, the AIBOC and the UFBU had staged many protests and agitations against the policies, which they consider to be against the principle of social banking. In 2012, another bill was tabled in the parliament called the Banking Law Amendment Bill providing certain liberalisations in the Banking Regulation Act and Bank Nationalisation Act.[54] The bill was opposed by the AIBOC and the UFBU. On the request of bank unions, many political parties opposed it as well and many MPs walked out on this issue. However, despite all these issues the bill was passed by the then government.

Despite the changes made in policies, the problem of banks have persisted. The problem of 'weak banks' has increased in the recent times. To solve this problem, the government has come up with recapitalisation plans, also called as called the turnaround plan, in which eleven banks have been identified where the future capital infusion would be conditional. These banks were IDBI Bank, Bank of India, UCO Bank, Andhra Bank, Indian Overseas Bank, Dena Bank, United Bank of India, Allahabad Bank, Bank of Maharashtra, Union Bank of India and Central Bank of India. The unions were asked to sign a memorandum of understanding (MoU) with the Ministry of Finance as precondition for this plan to be implemented. The AIBOC immediately called for a meeting on 24 March 2017 at Kolkata, where a detailed discussion happened and unions came to the conclusion that they were being asked to take responsibility for a turnaround whereas they have not been party to these decisions. Therefore, it was decided that the MoU would be signed only when government would agree that employee allowances would not be revised without consultation with respective unions.[55] Despite the pressure from the government, the unions stood firm and finally a revised MoU was signed on 28 March 2017. Above that, the AIBOC also prepared an alternative turnaround plan for each bank and also came up with another booklet called *Laudable*

Performance of Public Sector Banks – Facts and Lies, where they have suggested that huge amounts of NPAs are the real reason behind the bad performance of banks. Therefore, its recovery is an important condition for better performance of the banks.

To suggest an alternative for the better future of banking system in India, the AIBOC requested renowned economists C.P. Chandrasekhar and Jayati Ghosh to study the current challenges facing the banking industry and to suggest the alternatives. Therefore, a report was published in January 2018, where they suggested the way forward to solve the problems facing the banking industry. The report was submitted to members of parliament in the light of introduction of Financial Resolution and Deposit Insurance (FRDI) Bill and the continued attempt to privatise banks. The AIBOC analysed the FRDI bill and concluded that the provision of resolving authority in the bill could be very dangerous. The bill gives the resolution authority absolute powers and it can decide by itself to dissolve or merge banks. The resolution authority under the 'bail-in' clause was also given power not to give the depositors their money back and thus, tried to socialise the NPAs. Therefore, there has been a huge opposition to this bill. Apart from the books, seminars and discussions, the AIBOC also started a signature campaign. The AIBOC under the leadership of the present General Secretary also appeared before the Joint Parliamentary Committee, submitted a detailed presentation, and demanded rejection of the bill. Through all these efforts made by the AIBOC, the bill could not be passed in the parliament, yet.

The AIBOC is also making efforts to connect officers' movement to the larger working class movement. In this regard, the AIBOC has launched a new organisation called 'All India Public Sector and Central Government Officers Confederation', consisting of officers organisations in all public sector undertakings and Central Government Gazetted Officers' Confederation. They have launched campaign called 'Save Public Sector Forums'. TheAIBOC has also initiated 'People's parliament for unity and development', under which trade unions and diverse organisations of farmers, youth, women, NGOs and rights-based groups have jointly launched a national platform for debate on developmental issues. In regard, to increasing attack on public sector banks, the AIBOC had also launched a month long 'Save Public Sector – Save India' campaign in 2016. The campaign began with Kala Jatha (Street Play) and a short film at Chennai. On 5 June 2018, the AIBOC has released a book *Commendable Performance of Public Sector Banks 2017-2018.*

In the fight for better service conditions for the officers and to ensure ideal social banking, the AIBOC and its affiliates had to move to court in many occasions. On 28 August 2012, the officers organised a protest demonstration at the local head offices of the State Bank of India throughout the country on the demand of a five-day week work. In response to which, a letter was served to the General Secretaries advising them to not resort to such demonstrations in the future. Despite the reply by the SBIOA, the management went ahead with the enquiry proceedings. Against this move of the management, the officers had to go to court and filed an affidavit at the Madras High Court and other places. After prolonged hearings, the judgement was pronounced on 4 July 2013, which protected the right of officers to hold peaceful demonstration. This was a big victory for the officers against the management's high handedness.

The constant fight by the unions against the unilateralism by the managements have also led to many attacks on the organisations. In one case, the check-off facility by which subscriptions are given by individual members of the association are deducted at individual request directly from her/his salary was withdrawn. This facility was available to unions since 1975; therefore, against this arbitrary move of the management, SBIOA Chennai Circle and AISBOF approached the High Court of Madras. The Judgement was pronounced on 23 September 2013, in which the court ordered in favour of the unions.

> It is seen from the records that the check off facility extended to the petitioner association right from 1975 has been sought to be withdrawn and in fact, given effect on 17.09.013, especially, when similarly placed association, namely, Staff Union of State Bank of India, is enjoying the same benefit. It amounts to discrimination. Therefore, there shall be an order of interim stay as prayed for.

When the management did not implement the stay order, the AISBOF filed the contempt petition and Pratip Chaudhary, Chairman SBI, had to appear before the Madras Court and express regret.

Similarly, the IBA issued a letter to public sector banks on 7 April 2014 to withdraw the facility to cover travel abroad within the eligibility of leave fare concession within the country. Once again, the AISBOF and the AIBOC have filed a case at the Madras High Court for which a stay was granted. The AIBOC also filed a case against the government's move to collect Perquisite Tax from officers from 30 March 2010. The court has stayed the order, which was a great relief for officers in the banking sector. Another case filed by the AIBOC is regarding the appointment of the officers' and employee's director at the board of directors and the case is still going on.

Apart from the court cases on the issue of industrial relations in banking, the AIBOC has also filed cases on the issues related to larger societal concerns. One of them is the recent case filed by the AIBOC related to the Aadhar policy, where the AIBOC is a party to the case that is fighting for the right to privacy. The case is pending in the Supreme Court. Another important case filed by AIBOC is against the RBI circular dated 12 February 2018, changing the assets classification norms, which has increased the NPAs. Against this circular the AIBOC has approached the Delhi High Court. These are just a few of the legal cases fought by the AIBOC and its affiliates.

Development Work by the AIBOC

The developmental works taken up by the officers unions in

the banking sector sets them apart from other unions. It was E.A.G. Moses, who developed the concept of 'cradle to grave', that the organisation's role is to take care of its members for their whole life.[56] Cradle, here means the day one joins the banking industry and grave refers the person's association with the banking industry with banking industry, even after retirement. Basing its ideas on this thought, the unions in the banking sector industry have been involved in many non-bargaining and developmental activities like developing housing colonies, schools, and colleges among other things.

The Chennai circle association of the AISBOF, once demanded that there should be a provision of schools for the bank employees' children. However, the demand was not accepted by the bank management. Therefore, the association started a school on its own. Today, the SBIOA Chennai circle has twelve schools with more than 30,000 students enrolled.[58] Similarly, other federations of the AISBOF as well as the AIBOC itself has started schools in different parts of the country, where children of bank employees are given concessions. The trade union run schools also represent a model for a better schooling system. The Federal Bank Officers' Association runs the Federal Institute of Science and Technology (FISAT), which is one of the reputed institutes of India.

Apart from educational institutes, unions also have training institutions. The Federation of Bank of India Officers' Associations has one training institute called Foundation for United Trade Union Research & Education (FUTURE) and The All India State Bank Officers' Federation has 'National Academy of Trade Union Research and Education (NATURE).[59] These institutes train officers on disciplinary proceedings and are provided with the skills required for promotion as well. SBIOA, Chennai Circle has an institute SBIOA Institute for Trade Union Education and Research, which was the pioneer in this activity. Recently, many unions have also started coaching centres for aspirants to the banking sector. AISBOF, which is the biggest affiliate of the AIBOC, has organised various seminars in collaboration with Jawaharlal Nehru University and the proceedings have been published. One of the recent publications is *Alternative to Gyan Sangam Proposals*.

The unions in the banking sector also have housing colonies, which cater to the desire of officers to have their own house as it is becoming difficult for the middle class to own i own house. Here, again, the efforts of the Federal Bank Officers' Association have been pioneering, which has constructed a number of flats in different parts of Kerala.[61] Again, SBIOA Chennai circle has become a role model by constructing 1,875 flats as a gated community at Chennai, which was inaugurated by Rajnish Kumar, Chairperson of SBI in May 2018.

The discussion above shows that the banking industry and its employees, including its officers, are not only locked in a constant struggle with the managements that are constantly in an attempt to oppress them and to corner the larger share of the banks' profits, but after the implementation of the policies that heralded the beginning of the neoliberal regime in India, they are also engaged in the struggle with these policies and their ambassadors. Thus, the fight that the AIBOC has been leading is not only the fight for equal rights and better working conditions but also for dignity, and the preservation of the ideals of social banking, ideals which run counter to the principles of privatisation and neoliberalism. In order to counter the assault of neoliberalism and privatisation, the AIBOC along with other officers' unions have made a sincere attempt to implement the AIBOC's motto of taking care of the officers from 'the cradle to the grave'. The AIBOC led a movement for multiple developmental projects throughout the country, which is a culmination of these efforts to realise this slogan.

Notes

1. R.N. Godbole, ed., "Undeclared Emergency Grips Banks," *Common Bond*, January 1986, 1.
2. 'Loan Melas – Fake Applications Forms Being Sold in Open Market', *Common Bond*, May 1986, 4.
3. Ibid., 2.
4. «Premature Retirements – I.B.A.'s Version," *Common Bond*, February 1986, 7.

5. "Agitation Creates Impact – Government Holds Talks with the AIBOC," *Common Bond,* February 1986, 6.
6. "Regulation 20(1) Strikes Again," *Common Bond,* May 1986, 4.
7. "AIBOC Wins Case in Supreme Court," *Common Bond,* September 1989, 4.
8. R.N. Godbole, *Agitation by Officers of UCO Bank – Fraternal Support,* Circular No. 26 (Bangalore, Karnataka: All India Bank Officers' Confederation (AIBOC), 1988), 1.
9. R.N. Godbole, "Report of the General Secretary to the 2nd Session of General Council," *Common Bond,* January 1990, 29.
10. Ibid., 18.
11. S.R. Sen Gupta, "Report of the General Secretary to the 5th Session of General Council," *Common Bond,* January 1999, 18.
12. "Joint Action against the Move for Privatisation of Banks - Strike on 6th September 1991," *Common Bond,* September 1991, 1.
13. Ibid., 3.
14. "Fight against Privatisation to Continue," *Common Bond,* October 1991, 3.
15. Ibid.
16. "Memorandum Submitted to the Finance Minister," *Common Bond,* November 1991, 7.
17. Lawrence Saez. *Banking reform in India and China*. Springer, 2004, 44.
18. "Workshop on Narasimham Committee Report," *Common Bond,* March 1992, 11.
19. *Challenges and Strategies 1985-2010* (Bangalore, Karnataka: All India Bank Officers' Confederation (AIBOC), 2011), 19.
20. Ibid.,16.
21. ShanthaRaju (Former General Secretary of the AIBOC), interviewed by Sarika Chaudhary, Bangalore, India, February 2018.
22. S.R. Sen Gupta, "Report of the General Secretary to the 5th Session of General Council," *Common Bond,* January 1999, 17.
23. Ibid.
24. "UFBU Appears Before Narasimham Committee," *Common Bond,* April 1998, 1.
25. *Common Bond,* July 1998, p. 12, Vol. 17, No. 4
26. S.R. Sen Gupta, "Report of the General Secretary to the 5th Session of General Council," *Common Bond,* January 1999, 18.
27. S.R. Sen Gupta, "Report of the General Secretary to the 5th Session of General Council," *Common Bond,* January 1999, 18.
28. "Public Sector Banks Sought to be Termed as Weak," *Common Bond,* March 1999, 2.
29. "Government Releases Rs. 400 Crores Capital to UCO, UBI and Indian Bank," *Common Bond,* April 1999, 15.
30. Ibid.
31. "UFBU Meets Unions in UBI, UCO and India Bank," *Common Bond,* May 1999, 1.

32. "Tackling the Problem of Weak Banks," *Common Bond,* April 1999, 10.
33. "UFBU Meets Verma Committee," *Common Bond,* June 1999, 4.
34. "Verma Committee Report – Categorisation of Public Sector Banks," *Common Bond,* November 1999, 4.
35. Ibid.
36. "Verma's Explosion," *Common Bond,* November 1999, 1.
37. "UFBU Delegation Meets RBI Governor," *Common Bond,* December 1999, 2.
38. "Joint Struggle Committee of Financial Sector Union," *Common Bond,* December 1999, 5.
39. Ibid.
40. "Morcha to LIC at Pondicherry," *Common Bond,* January 2000, 9.
41. "AIBOC Executive Committee Meets at Calcutta," *Common Bond,* April 2000, 2.
42. "UCO, UBI Emit Revival Sparks," *Common Bond,* August 2000, 6.
43. Ibid., 6.
44. "Privatisation Bill Introduced in Parliament," *Common Bond,* December 2000, 1.
45. Ibid.
46. Ibid., 2.
47. Ibid.
48. Jayati Ghosh, C.P. Chandrasekhar, and Prabhat Patnaik, *Demonetisation Decoded: A Critique of Indias Currency Experiment* (Milton: Taylor and Francis, 2017).
49. Harvinder Singh (Former General Secretary of the AIBOC), interviewed by Sarika Chaudhary, Bangalore, India, June 2018.
50. Ibid.
51. C.P. Chandrasekhar and Jayati Ghosh, *Indian Banking - Current Challenges and Alternatives for the Future* (New Delhi: Economic Research Foundation, 2018), 1.
52. *Challenges and Strategies 1985-2010* (Bangalore, Karnataka: All India Bank Officers' Confederation (AIBOC), 2011), 55.
53. "Independent Commission on Banking and Financial Policy," *Common Bond,* April 2000, 2.
54. D.S. Rishabadas, *Be Ready for Instant Strike against Banking Law Amendment Bill,* Circular No. 70 (Bangalore, Karnataka: All India Bank Officers' Confederation (AIBOC), 2012).
55. D.T. Franco, *Press Release,* PDF, the AIBOC, March 4, 2017.
56. D.T. Franco (Current Secretary General of the AIBOC), interviewed by Sarika Chaudhary, Bangalore, India, May 2018.
57. Ibid.
58. Ibid.
60. Ibid.
61. Ibid.

Afterword

The documentation of the history of All India Bank Officers' Confederation provides some lessons for the organisation of the managerial and supervisory class of workers. It shows the importance of the recognition of this class as 'workers'. As the discussion in the preceding chapters has shown, the process of instilling a working class consciousness amongst the bank officers was the result of long and continuous struggle and organisation building. This process influenced by the developments in the larger working class movement from the pre-independence era, especially through the unionization of the clerical staff of banks. We can therefore surmise through this history that the organisation of one section of the working class can have a positive impact on another section, even though its class interests may be substantially different from the mass of the proletariat.

The second important lesson from the story of the AIBOC is that the formation of unions is not merely for the self-interests of its members. Rather, unionization should be done with the broader objective of bringing about worker friendly transformations within the larger industrial structure. The AIBOC's ongoing struggle for inclusive public sector banking and its outreach work in education and livelihood illustrates the multi-pronged strategy that can be adopted by working class organisations under the contemporary scenario. The perspective that informs these actions perceives the AIBOC as a catalyst in supporting the struggles of women, farmers, students and other section of the society. It also demonstrates that middle class white collar worker unions can have an important role to play in the larger working class movement.

The evolution of a democratic organizational set up has been central to the success that the AIBOC has achieved in expansion of its organisation. As shown in this book, the expansion is not only in terms of organizing bank officers in public sector banks, but also in attracting new sections of the population. The organisation of women, youth and employees of regional and private sector banks was instrumental in making the AIBOC a militant movement. The youth convention and women convention are definitely a way forward.

At another level, the advocacy of the AIBOC regarding policy issues has taken a new turn with the present day labour and financial sector reforms. The setting up of the people's parliament process, national level conventions with mainstream trade unions and workers organisations, studies on the impact of reforms on rural and urban poor, etc., have demonstrated the AIBOC's potential to provide inputs to the larger democratic struggle. Thus the role of the AIBOC becomes crucial in the emerging scenario. By meeting this challenge successfully the AIBOC will show that the interest of the union of a managerial class is not necessarily contrary to goals of the larger working class movement at the current conjecture.

Annexures

Annexure 1: Exchange of letters between Samar Mukherjee (MP, CPI (M)) and H.M. Patel (Finance Minister 1977-1980) on the issue of implementation of the Pillai Committee Recommendations.

Shri H.M Patel, Union Finance Minister replies to Shri Samar Mukherjee— Letter No. 1985/FM/78/VIP(1) dt. July, 3. 1978

Dear Shri Mukherjee,

Please refer to your letter dated 4th June and 23rd June and the enclosures sent along with regarding implementation of Pillai Committee Report.

You must have already read in the papers that I met representatives of the AICOBOO (All India Confederation of Bank Officers' Organisation) recently in response to their representation to me. As it has been decided that IBA (Indian Banks' Association) will discuss further with the AICOBOO various specified points raised by it.

I would like to assure you at the same time that Pillai Committee Scheme is not against the interest of Bank Officers". Pillai Committee Scheme seeks to bring about a standardisation the salary structure and allowances of officers of different nationalised banks. Such standardisation already exists in respect of workmen staff of Nationalised banks. You will agree that there should be uniformity in the pay scales, allowances and perquisite being drawn by officers doing the same kind of job in banks under the common ownership.

By and large, the grades prescribed under the Pillai Committee Scheme are much better than prevailing in the* Banking industry. In effect, it would mean more contributory provident fund better gratuity, better house rent allowance, more medical benefits to most of the bank officers. In terms of pay fixation, the formula is such that at the junior level, officers would get at least one increment and at the other levels also there would be some increase on figment. In any case, the pay and dearness allowance drawn by an officer are protected. In respect of allowances and there are any number of them in banks at present such as post allowance, duty allowance, onerous duty allowance, closing allowance, vault custodian allowance, transfer allowance, hill and fuel allowance, personal allowance, etc. Naturally some measure of rationalisation has been brought about. Even here, the difference between the allowances admissible and those drawn is to be protected by way of personal allowance to officers. Perquisites such as free car and driver, free furniture and furnishings, concessional loans for purchase of consumer goods, winter clothing, etc. are of course sought to be reduced or done away with as it is felt that these are anachronistic in the pattern of society we are seeking to bring into being.

The D. A. Pattern also is sought to be brought in line with the general D. A. pattern prevailing in Government and public sector undertaking by and large. The pay scale of junior most bank officers in Rs. 700-1800 which is equivalent to at least three grades of any class-I service in the Government. At its highest scale, the bank officers, excluding the chairman and Managing Directors, are in Rs. 3000-125-3500 scale which is what top civil servant in the Government expect. It also compares favourably both top positions in public sector enterprises. What is more, it is advantageous to the present incumbent to continue to remain in his present scale and draw his existing allowances, he is given an option to do till such time as he is promoted.

I have mentioned all this at length because there is a general misunderstanding, that by implementing the pillai Committee's scheme we would be drastically reducing the emoluments of the officers. This is far from true. Actually it is estimated that consequent upon the implementation of the Pillai Committee Scheme all the nationalised banks put together may have to spend at least an additional sum of Rs. 8 to 10 crores, which obliviously means that something more is being given rather than being taken away from the officers.

I hope this reassures you that by implementing the Pillai Committee Scheme we are not only trying to do away with an anachronistic and wasteful perquisites and allowances but are at the same time giving to the officers a better wage structure, more terminal benefits and reasonable and uniform perquisites and allowances.

Kind regards,

Your Sincerely

sd/-

(H.M. PATEL)

* * *

Mukherjee writes back

Shri Patel,

Kindly refer to your letter No. 1985FM/78 VIP (I) dated 3, 1978 addressed to me regarding, the grievances of Bank Officers.

I do not agree with your views expressed in the letter. Apart from the fact that the terms and conditions as proposed by the Pillai Committee and subsequently modified by the Study Group of bankers headed by Shri P.F. Gutta and Govt. executives are prejudicial to the interest of Bank Officers as would be evident from the enclosed booklet, the Bank Officers are more concerned about their hard earned trade union rights which were intended to be taken away by the Govt. of India by imposing unilaterally the said terms and conditions in the name of standardisation. In fact, more than any monetary considerations, Bank Officers have been struggling only for protection of their fundamental trade union rights of collective bargaining. In fact, the Officers have been demanding that any change in their existing service condition should be settled bilaterally with the practice ever since the Bank Officers organised themselves into a trade union body.

The standardisation made for other employees in the Bank also done through two awards, viz. Sastri Award and Desai Award and subsequently through bilateral talks in 1966 and 1970 and not through unilateral impositions. It would, therefore, be evident that the standardisation for other employees were achieved through stages and not overnight as is being contemplated for Bank officers.

From the above, it is clear that the struggles of the Bank officers is quite justified. However, I am glad that you had decided to intervene and the bipartite negotiation, between the Indian Banks' Association and the AICOBOO the representative body of the all Bank Officers have resumed. The Bank Officers have always been striving to arrive at an amicable settlement of all the problems through bilateral negotiation. But unfortunately it is the Management which tried to by-pass this time tested procedure by trying to impose the so-called Pillai Committee's recommendations on the officers.

However, I am hopeful the present negotiation will conclude on a happy note.

With regards,

Your Sincerely

Sd/-

(Samar Mukherjee)

Annexure 2: Letter written by R.N. Godebole as the convenor of the negotiating committee of the AICOBOO on the issue of wage revision.

Text of Our Letter 18/466/85 Dt. 27th June 85
Addressed to the Chairman. I.B.A.

Dear Sir.

Revision of Terms and conditions of Service of the Bank Officers:

Please refer to the discussions at this meeting between representatives of I.B.A. and the members of the Negotiating Committee of AICOBOO held on 24-6-85 St Bombay.

You were good enough to convey to the AICOBOO, the decisions of this Government on the proposals for revision, evolved through bipartite discussions between I.B.A. and AICOBOO, at several meetings held during 1984. After obtaining clarifications from you on various aspects, we slated that an objective assessment of this proposals is modified by the Government will be made by us and that based on such assessment we shall convey our reaction to you. Our Action Committee met Bombay on 26th and 26th June 1985. On s thorough analysis of all the circumstances relating to the formulation of proposals through bipartite discussions between I.B.A. and AICOBOO and the modifications made by the Government, the Committee expressed the following views :

(a) The Government has made very substantial modifications in the proposals. It is difficult to understand or explain, the relevance of I.B.A. in the determination of terms and conditions of service of bank Officers. I.B.A. was entrusted by the Government the responsibility of holding talks with representatives of bank Officers, on salary revision and making recommendations 10 the Government. It was assumed that I.B.A. was acting on the basis of some brief from the Government, atleast in essential areas. Did I.B.A. act outside the brief or was no brief given by the Government or did the Government go back on its brief, are all questions that are arising, in the context that right from the BP structure. DA. Scheme, House Rent Scheme, to the date of effect, the Government, has made sweeping changes. In other words instead of clearing the proposals submitted by I.B.A. the Government has returned entirely a new set of proposals. This very adversely reflects on the image of I.B.A. as a professional body representing the bank managements in negotiations with the representative organisations of Officers. It also sets at naught the principle of mutuality of interests between I.B.A. and the Officers' Organisation, which AICOBOO holds has to be the basis for Interaction, consultation and negotiation between the two parties.

AICOBOO does not deny that the Government has the right of final decision in the matter. Notwithstanding the existence of the right, it is submitted the right cannot be and should not be exercised by the Government arbitrarily. It would have been in fitness of the things if the Government had remitted the proposals beck to I.B.A. with their advices or guidelines end I.B.A. had held further discussions with the Officers' Organisations for the purpose of modifying the proposals, by mutual agreement. Alternatively a tripartite meeting of I.B.A , Officers' Organisations and the Government, should have been celled. None of these things have been done. The result is several gaps remain in the proposals, end the bank Officers end their Organisations are left dissatisfied. Promotion of goodwill and mutuality of interests, which should be the aim of salary revision, have received least consideration at the hands of the Government. The Committee therefore desires to convey 10 the IB.A. its strong sentiments over the situation that has developed, over the actions of the Government and more particularly over the inability of I.B.A. to defend its own professional views and convictions.

(b) Without prejudice to the above basic stand, the proposals made by the Government were examined.

(c) We disagree with (i) reduction of one stage in Scale-I and (ii) retention of E.B. in Scale I

(d) We wish to drew attention to the paltry increases in terms of B.P. end D.A. available at stages 8 and 9 of Scale-I. With higher recovery of Provident fund. the net take-home pay at these stages stands reduced as a consequence of REVISION.

Existing Position

Stage	*BP*	*DA*	*Total*	*PF*	*Take Home Pay*
8	1000	1516	2516	83	2433
9	1050	1506	2556	87	2489

After Revision

BP	*DA*	*Total*	*PF*	*Take Home Pay*
1615	948	2563	135	2428(–5)
1685	948	2633	140	2493(+24)

(e) The anomaly in the D.A. scheme, whereby D.A. drops at the basic pay stage of Rs. 1,615, thereafter it is fist between basic stages of Rs. 1,615 and Rs. 2,376 and then rises again has been perpetuated. Thus one unfortunate group of Officers drawing basic pay between Rs. 1,615 and Rs. 2,375 will get lower O.A. than their Juniors as well as their Seniors in the same scale. This issue was raised by us as far back as in 1983. I.B.A. took up the matter with the Government and we were later assured that the anomaly would be rectified at the time of revision. That this anomaly should be rectified atleast prospectively from the date of revision, if not retrospectively was accepted by the IB.A. The proposes now made are not consistent with the earlier assurances of I.B.A.

(f) Workman drawing basic pay between Rs. 1,196 and Rs. 1,630 get D.A. adjustments with rise or foil of 4 points in index, whereas Officers drawing basic pay within the same range (Rs. 1,175 to 1,645) will not be entitled for adjustment on the basis of 4 points cycle. While there should be uniform cycle of 4 points for all employees and Officers, atleast at parallel pay ranges, discrimination should not have been made.

(g) The group of Officers presently coming within different cycles is as under :

8 points 1001-1600 Scale I

16 points 1601-2400 Scales I, II, III & IV

24 points 2401 & above Scales V.VI8VII

On revision, the grouping would be as under:

8 points 1176-1600 Scale-I

16 points 1601-2425 Scales 1 & II 24 points 2426 & above Scales II, III, IV, V, VI & VII

If at all multi-cycle system is to be retained, then for equity and rationality, the cycles must be as under :-

CYCLE:	PAY-RANGE :
4 points	1175-1616 Scale-I
8 points	1685-3450 Scales-II, III, IV
16 points	3461 & above Scales. V, VI & VI

(h) In any case D.A. payable at the stage beyond Rs. 1,580 (where the maximum is reached) should not be lower than the D.A. calculated at the notional basic pay of Rs. 1,580.

The H.R.A. scheme conceived by the Government is not clear even to Indian Banks' Association. The proposals agreed to by AICOBOO with Indian Banks' Association were on en assumption that payment of house rent allowance at rates specified, would be a part of compensation system and not by way of subsidy. If it is to be a subsidy towards expenditure incurred on rent by the

Officers over and above 10% of their basic pay, AICOBOO would insist upon higher rates as well as higher ceilings as under:

Class-I -	25%	Maximum	Rs. 800/-
Class-II -	20%	Maximum	Rs. 600/-
Class-III -	15%	Maximum	Rs. 500/-
Class-IV -	10%	Maximum	Rs. 500

(i) Officers in Reserve Bank of India are entitled to H.R.A as a part of the compensation system. Only where Officers are provided with quarters or leased housing accommodation, they are required to surrender the H.R.A. This system, which was obtaining in Banks, prior to implementation of Pillal Committee Recommendations, must be restored the small concession shown by the government of limiting the recovery towards quarters leased house, at 10% of first stage in the scale (and not grade) is not at all satisfactory.

(k) The proposals do not spell out whether the basic pay celling of Rs. 1,059 for payment of H.R.A. without production of rent receipts, would be proportionately raised to Rs. 1,700.

More than anything else the Committee expressed greatest disappointment over the fixation of the date of effect for the proposals as 1-7-84 as against 1-7-83 in the case of workmen in the same banking industry. The reason of alleged low-profitability of banks, is not at all convincing. The low profitability of the banks, is mainly due to the policies or the Government of opening branches in rural areas. These branches are opened for the purpose of extending service and not for making profits. The other major factor influencing profitability of banks, is the monetary measures adopted by the R.B I. for regulating credit. In these circumstances why should their bank Officers alone be penalized for the so called low profitability of banks? If the banks can bear the load of revision prospectively for Officers, if they can bear the load for workmen retrospectively from 1-7-83, it is illogical and unbelievable that the banks cannot bear the load in case of Officers for just one year period from 1-7-83 to 1 7-84; instead of totally denying revision from 1-7-83, the Government could have proposed staggering payment, to distribute the load over one or two more years.

No consideration has been given to the lot of Officers who retired between 1-7-83 and 1-7-84.

By giving effect to revision from 1-7-84 these unfortunate persons have been deprived of gratuity amount to the extent of Rs. 15.000/-. A clerk who retired during the same period got the benefit of the revised basic pay for the purpose of computation of gratuity.

Officers who retired between 1-7-83 and 1-7-84 as also those in service, suffered loss of provident fund contribution for the period, as result of unjustifiable action of the Government in delaying the date of effect by one year.

Employees promoted from clerical cadre to Officers cadre, are aggrieved by not getting any compensation on promotion at all. On the other hand contribution to Provident Fund has been reduced as a result of promotion. The proposals do not make it clear whether some minimum deferential would be assured to promotees of this dark period.

Officers have been smarting under the humiliation of drawing lower salary than their subordinates. They were only hoping that their scales also would be revised retrospectively from 1-7-83 and amends would comeforth. By the Government's decision not to give effect from 1-7-83, the wound end scar would be permanent.

Quite e number of Officers have been drawing adjusting and personal allowances even now just to protect the emoluments, which they were drawing prior to implementation of Pillai committee Recommendations. There is no clarity how these allowance would be treated. As in the of workmen these allowance's also need to be consolidated.

No final decision has been given either by the Government or the Indian Banks' Association on the following issues :

a) Extension of the new scales to the Officers in Private Sector Banks.

b) Stagnation increments.

c) CAIIB allowance after an Officer reaches maximum in the scale.

d) Fitment Formula on promotion from clerical cadre to Officers' cadre and method of assuring minimum differential on promotion.

e) Formula for fitment on promotion from one Scale in Officers' cadre to another scale, taking into account factor of higher recovery towards housing accommodation, an Officer would be required to pay, with reference to the 1st stage in the higher scale to which he is promoted

f) Conveyance Loans—higher celling for Cora.

g) Post Allowances—Differing Responsibility levels within the same scale

h) Travailing and Halting Allowances improvement in the present scales:

i) Closing Allowances—higher exiling.

j) Officiating Allowances/Deputation Allowance—revision and rationalization.

k) Project Allowance—revision.

l) Hill—Fuel Allowance—revision.

m) Special Area Allowances—revision

n) Discomfort Allowance—revision.

o) Education Allowance—Mid-academic transfer Allowance—revision of terms.

p) Leave Fare Concession - liberalizations of terms and conditions - payment in lieu of the facility if not availed.

q) Leave Encystment - Payment of full emoluments.

We wish to convey that on all the counts, namely processes of negotiation delay in finalization, denial of effect from 1-7-83. curtailment of due increases at various levels of scale end continuation of anomalous D.A. Scheme, considerable dissatisfaction has been caused amongst the bank Officers. As a matter of fact. Officers in Scale I between stages 2 to 13 do not get by way of final revision, increases even equal to the interim relief granted by the government to its employees. Officers in Scale VI and VII also get far lower increases in comparison to the interim relief granted by the Government to its Officers.

We finally urge upon the Government and Indian Banks' Association to reconsider the matte, and afford relief for distortions, inadequacies and anomalies referred to in foregoing paragraphs and also to convene a bipartite meeting immediately to discuss the residual issues and finalise the revision in other terms and conditions of services so that it may be possible to appraise the package in total.

We look forward to hearing from you as early as possible. We do hope that the seriousness of the situation and the possible effects of the non-settlement of the problems on the industrial relations in the industry, would be given due consideration by you and that you would respond in a manner as to reduce tensions and promote harmony.

Thanking you,

Yours Sincerely,

Sd/-

(R.N. GODBOLE)
Vice-President
and Convenor, Negotiating committee.

Annexure 3: Some of the resolutions passed in first General Council of the AIBOC

Bonus

The General Council of All India Bank Officers' Confederation meeting in its FIRST SESSION at Hyderabad from 16th,17th and 18th December 1986 welcomes the recent amendment to Payment of Bonus Act, widening the scope of definition of the term employees to include all employees drawing salary or wages upto Rs. 2,500. The meeting also welcomes the amendment to the Act made in September 1985 to enhance the ceiling on wages for computation of bonus to Rs. 1,600. The Council would however like to call urgent attention of the Government and the Bank Managements to the anomalous situation that has arisen in the matter of bonus as between the employees drawing wages upto Rs. 2,500 and those drawing wages marginally above Rs. 2,500. A slab increase in Dearness. Allowance, transfer to CCA area or accrual of annual increment renders employees drawing wages marginally below Rs. 2,500 , totally ineligible for bonus, causing a reduction in average monthly emoluments inclusive of bonus component. The meeting urges that this anomaly be rectified.

2. The meeting would also like to record that despite the two amendments referred to herein-before, more than 90% of the Bank Officers are still outside the purview of the Bonus Act. The internal relativity in wages in the banking Industry is very finely balanced. In fact quite a number of officers promoted from ranks continue to draw, the same emoluments as they would have drawn if they were not promoted. The bonus element distorts this fine balance and acts as a serious disincentive to clerical staff in accepting promotion to the cadre of officers. The Banking Industry depends upon the internal promotions to fill up at least 80% of the posts of officers. Therefore it is necessary to preserve the existing incentives for promotion and to the extent possible improve them.

3. Since time immemorial officers of almost all the banks were receiving bonus on the same basis as workmen. In 1975

the Bonus Act was amended to exclude Banking Industry from its purview. Under some alleged direction of the Government, the Management stopped payment of Bonus to the Officers, though as a matter of fact, the Officers, derived their right to Bonus, not so much from the Bonus Act, as from the custom. The enactment of Bonus Act in 1965 or its amendment in 1975, did not really affect the right of the officers to the customary Bonus.

4. It was the fond hope of the officers, that the Government would review the position and that the status quo ante in the matter of bonus would be restored and the officers would get back their right to bonus It is a matter of regret that the unfair discrimination brought about in 1975 still continues and a very large section of officers continues to be denied Bonus.

5. The Council calls to the attention of the government, that Bonus has now been widely recognized as deferred wage. In that sense every person who earns a wage, by whatever name called as long as it is a price for his labour, is entitled for the deferred wage namely the bonus. Exclusion of officers or employees drawing salary above Rs. 2,500 for the purpose of Bonus is inconsistent with the definition of Bonus as deferred wage.

6. Even if the Bonus is defined as sharing of profits between the employers and employees, on the considerations, that it is the labour of the worker which contributes to the profits, every employee, irrespective of salary, rank, class or designation, if he contributes to the profit, should be entitled to his share of profit, namely the Bonus. Classification of employees otherwise than on this basis, namely whether or not they contribute to profits, is absolutely Incorrect, illogical, discriminatory and unfair.

7. The Council urges upon the Government to immediately take steps to amend the Bonus Act to end discrimination against the employees and officers drawing salary above Rs. 2,500.

8. The law permits the Banks not to disclose their profits. The scheme of the Bonus Act, which is based on disclosed profits alone, is heavily loaded against the Bank employees and officers. In the present context of majority of Banks

being in public sector, the anachronism of special rights to Banks from disclosing their true financial position is pot at all necessary. The ownership of the state, more than the financial soundness of the Banks, assures public confidence in Banks. It is therefore only right that the Banks should be compelled to disclose their correct profits, and pay the legitimate share of the profits to its employees and officers. However if it is still felt necessary to continue the protection given to the Banks for other public purposes, to ensure that atleast the protection is not at the cost of the employees and officers, the system of computation of gross profit, should be appropriately modified and due opportunities given to the employees and officers to verify the profit figures. Alternatively, freedom should bo given to the Bank Managements to negotiate the Bonus issue outside the purview of the Bonus Act and its limitations, taking into account the industrial relations, the need to maintain the morale of the employees and to provide incentive.

9. The Council directs that all steps be taken to give expression to the feelings of the officers on the issue of Bonus, to canvass opinion at all the necessary quarters in favour of the officers' case, and to strive by all legitimate means, in coordination With other Organisations, to get justice in the matter of bonus to the Officers.

* * *

Security Arrangements

The General Council of the All India Bank Officers' Confederation meeting in its 1st Session at Hyderabad from 16th, 17th and 18th December 1986 commiserates and condoles with the families and dependents of employees, Officers and Bank Customers who have been victims of dacoities and robberies at various branches of the bank in the country in recent times. The Council expresses its deep anguish and concern over this growing threat and menace not only to the banks and their employees but to the Society at large.

2. Show and decor of the bank buildings have received precedence over internal security arrangements at quite a number of branches-. This trend should be reversed. Security of Cash, valuables and more particularly invaluable lives of employees, must be the prime consideration of the Managements of Banks. The Council calls upon the Managements to review and strengthen the internal security arrangements in all the branches.

3. The Council is aware that given law and order situation in the country, no amount of security arrangements such as alarm systems or posting of armed guards can prevent dacoities and robberies. These have therefore become the regular job-hazards of the bank employees and Officers. To face these job-hazards, morale of employees should be high. Every effort should be made by the Managements and the Government to maintain the morale of the bank employees and officers.

4. Compensation to the families of employees injured or killed in an incident of dacoity or robbery, should not be in the nature of 'charity' but should be a recognition of the supreme sacrifice the employee has made. It should be adequate as a social security measure to the dependents enabling them to maintain the same standard of living.

5. Payment of adequate cash compensation, employment of one of the dependents, writing off of housing/conveyance and other loans and such superannuation benefits as the employee may have received if he had completed full term of service, need to be considered. The Council urges upon the Government and the Managements to give their urgent attention to this matter.

* * *

Five-Day-Week

The General Council of the All India Bank Officers' Confederation meeting in its 1st Session at Hyderabad from 16th to 18th December 1986 is of the opinion that the step taken by the Central Government and some of the State Governments to introduce 5-day week, is a step in the right direction. The

Council is satisfied that the measure will lead to efficiency, economy and better functioning of the organizational systems of the Government and afford necessary leisure to the employees.

The General Council demands that 5-day week concept be uniformly introduced in the industrial sector and more particularly in the banking industry.

* * *

Computerisation

The General Council of All India Bank Officers' Confederation meeting in its 1st Session at Hyderabad from 16th, 17th and 18th December 1986, notes with concern the manner in which computerisation is being hustled in the banks. The introduction of computers has far reaching effects in the control systems in the banks with which Officers are directly concerned. Yet the Managements or the Government have not thought it necessary or fit to hold consultations with the Officers' Organisations on the subject. Despite huge expenditure on purchase of computers and on engaging consultants, the system is not working properly. Therefore duplication of computer work and manual work has become inevitable.

The General Council finds itself unable to support the scale of computerisation contemplated in the banking industry. The Council apprehends that the computerisation mis-adventure will cause serious unemployment problems in the country and undermine the delicately poised economy.

The Council urges upon the Managements to go slow with the computerisation, to redefine the areas of responsibility of the Officers and in any case not to proceed with further computerisation, without consultations with the Confederation. The Council warns that if the Managements ignore the basic issues raised herein, AIBOC would be compelled to resort to appropriate collective actions in coordination and collaboration with other trade union organisations in the banking industry, similarly disposed, towards the Computer menace.

* * *

Delinking of Associate Banks

The General Council of All India Bank Officers' Confederation meeting in its 1st session at Hyderabad from 16th to 18th December 1986 endorses the demand made by the Associate Banks Officers' Association for ending the subsidiary status of the Associate Banks and for constituting these Banks as Government owned Banks on the same basis as the 20 Nationalised Banks. The considerations behind making State Bank of India the holding Bank for the 7 small Banks, which had some relevance in 1959, has lost its validity altogether in the wake of recent developments. The last batch of nationalisation sow the Government taking over 6 banks whose deposits were above Rs. 200 crores. All these banks now enjoy an independent status as fully owned Government Banks.

Each of the 7 Associate Banks has aggregate deposits for higher than Rs.200 crores. It is therefore anomalous and unfair to prolong the subsidiary status of these banks, when Banks much smaller in size have already become autonomous units in the Public Sector. This Council firmly believes that if the Associate Banks are given autonomous status, there is vast potential for their growth and development. As independent banks they can play their legitimate role, far better, in the nation's tasks of accelerating economic growth.

This Council urges upon the Government to bring in immediate legislation for transfer of ownership of the Associate Banks to the Central Government for constituting them into separate banking units.

* * *

Conduct And Discipline Rules

The General Council of the All India Bank Officers' Confederation meeting in its 1st Session.at Hyderabad from 16th, 17th and 18th December 1986 demands that the Conduct and Discipline Rules which are a legacy of imperialist regime, be scrapped and that rules which are based on trust in the employees which presume good faith on the part of the employees and which seek to promote a culture of self-discipline, be introduced.

The Council calls upon the Bank Managements to initiate dialogue with the Confederation immediately for the purpose of framing such rules.

* * *

Special Area Compensatory Allowances

The General Council of All India Bank Officers' Confederation meeting in its 1st session at Hyderabad from 16th to 18th December 1936 stresses the need to compensate the employees posted to high-altitude areas, border-areas, very interior rural areas, tribal areas and other difficult centres for hardships suffered by them, for high cost of living at these centres and for double establishments they are compelled to maintain in the interest of the education of children, medicare of the dependents etc.

The General Council strongly feels that the selection of centres which should qualify as difficult areas and the quantum of compensation payable to the officers posted at such centres, should be independent of whether or not the Central Government or State Government pay any special area allowances to their employees at the respective centres or the rate at which the Governments pay the allowances. There are very substantial and material differences in the employment under the banking service and in Civil Service. Compensation systems and responsibility structures also widely differ. Transfer, placement and promotion Systems are very much divergent. Banks have been entrusted the task of expanding the branch network in these extremely difficult areas. The banks have been able to perform their part extremely well because of the cooperation and the spirit of sacrifice shown by the officers. However as the banks have neglected to recognise the human element factor and have failed to attend to the genuine hardships of the officers, frustration has set in among the officers. The Banks will have to create climate and motivation by which Officers would volunteer to work in the difficult areas. First step towards this in to fix reasonable special compensatory allowances to officers posted at difficult areas.

The Council demands that Officers serving in difficult areas should have an option to take up, at the cost of the banks, residential accommodation for their families at a convenient centre where education and medical facilities of the required standard are available.

The Council urges upon the Management to commence immediate dialogue with the Confederation on the subject and settle the issue to the mutual satisfaction of both the parties.

* * *

Appointment of Consultants

The General Council of All India Bank Officers1 Confederation meeting in its 1st session at Hyderabad on 16th, 17th and 18th December 1986, notes that there is a growing trend amongst the Public Sector Banks to engage the services of experts and consultants in various fields. The Banks have developed and specialised their officers in fields like financing of agriculture, small scale industries, large scale industries, and overseas, operations. Besides training the general staff in special areas, the banks have recruited on regular basis specialist staff in Engineering, Computers, Law, Security, Industrial Relations, Taxation and various other fields. It is therefore difficult to comprehend why the banks should need consultants in these areas. Remuneration and/or fees and perquisites disproportionate to the services needed or rendered are given by the Banks to the Consultants. Several irregular practices are reported in appointment and fixation of terms of appointment of such consultants.

The Council suggests that the power to engage Consultants and to fix their remuneration should be centralised and all appointments with their tenure, purpose, remuneration should be published through banks' circulars. This system will establish bonafides and will give no room for allegations.

The Council calls upon the Managements to publish the details of the current assignments given to the Consultants with all details.

Annexure 4: Letter written by the AIBOC to the Chairpersons of all the Regional Rural banks on the issue of pay parity.

Text of AIBOC's letter no. 1201/348/87 dated 13 July 1987 addressed to the Chairmen of all the Regional Rural Banks

Revision of Terms and Conditions of Services of the Officers

Dear Sir.

We represent the officers of RRBs set up in different states under the RRB Act 1976. We are also the principal bargaining agents for the Officers of all commercial banks.

The Executive Committee of our Organisation, which met at Delhi on 13th and 14th June noted with deep concern that the terms and conditions of service of the officers of RRBs are not in tune with the position obtaining in the banking industry, though officers of RRBs perform the same functions as officers of commercial banks. This apart, as between the RRBs themselves there is no uniformity in the conditions of service of the officers. The salaries and conditions of service of the officers in quite a number of RRBs are very much sub-standard. The committee therefore resolved that a requisition be made, to the authorities duly empowered by the RRB Act to determine the terms and conditions of service of the officers, to immediately consider the question of revision of the terms and conditions of Service. Under Section 17 of RRB Act read with Section 8 thereof, the Board of Directors is empowered to appoint such number of employees and officers as may be necessary and to determine the terms and conditions of their service.

We therefore send this requisition to you. We also enclose a copy of the Charter of Demands adopted by the Executive Committee. We request you to place this letter along with the Charter of Demands before the Board of Directors of your Bank at the earliest possible opportunity.

It is a good practice for the Managements to involve employees/officers in the process of determination of terms and conditions of service of the respective groups. Such co-determination of conditions of service leads to harmonious relations, goodwill and higher productivity. We do hope your Board of Directors will appreciate the merit of the Bipartite System and adopt the good practice in the context of the revision of terms and conditions of service of the officers for which requisition is made by us on behalf of the officers of your Bank.

We await your early response in the matter.

Thanking you.

Yours faithfully,

(R.N. GODBOLE)
General Secretary

Annexure 5: Resolutions passed in the second General Council of the AIBOC on the issues of communal harmony and working class unity.

Communal Harmony and National Integration

The General Council of the All India Bank Officers' Confederation meeting in its 2nd Triennial Session at Ahmedabad from 16th to 18th December 1989 expresses its distress at communal violence periodically erupting in different parts of the country. The communal frenzy has claimed several innocent lives, rendered several children orphans and destroyed several homes, in the recent past.

The unity and integrity of the nation is seriously threatened by the fissiparous tendencies of communalism. fundamentalism and acts of anti-social elements exploiting religious sentiments and fanning communal hatred.

The Council solemnly prays to all the people to show tolerance and forbearance towards their brethren belonging to another religion or community. Establishment of a secular state is the sacred goal of the Constitution. Every citizen has a duty, to translate this into reality and ensure peace and freedom to all.

The Council pledges itself to strive without respite to create amity between all people of the country and to promote and maintain unity and integrity of the nation. It calls upon all its members to be missionaries in this national goal.

* * *

Working Class Unity

The General Council of All India Bank Officers' Confederation meeting in its 2nd Triennial Session at Ahmedabad form 16th 18lh December 1989, expresses its anguish over the splintering of the trade unions in several industries and establishments. The main reason for the phenomenon is that quite a number of the unions are affiliated to or controlled by one or the other political party. Political parties have a tendency to split on ideological grounds or due to leadership ambitions, groupism or personal conflicts. When a political party splits, the trade unions affiliated to it or controlled by it are also afflicted by the same syndrome. Internal rivalries, poor performance of the leadership and instigations by the Management, have also led to splits in the unions. Resulting multiplicity of unions has only weakened the working class movement.

The Council calls upon all the unions to whichever colour they belong and whichever category they represent namely blue collar, while collar, supervisory/managerial or technical, to ponder over the situation, shed superficial differences and direct their attention to the main goal viz working class unity and march in unison towards a new era of total unity of all wage earners.

Annexure 6: Resolutions on the recommendations of the Narasimham Committee passed the third General Council.

Narasimham Committee

The All India Bank Officers' Confederation meeting in its 3rd Triennial Session at Agra on 16th, 17th & 18.1 h December 1992 notes that the hidden agenda of the Committee appointed by the Government under the Chairmanship of Shri M. Narasimham tor the purpose o! Study of the existing structure, procedure and functioning of all the Financial Institutions was to get an alibi tor privatisation of the State Sector Banks, The Committee has very faithfully submitted the directed report. The Committee has recommended slashing of the credit to the priority sector, so that more resources are available to the big industrial houses. The Committee wants the Banks to stop branch expansion in rural areas. It has recommended gradual withdrawal of Nationalised Banks from the rural scene In effect, the Committee wants the Nationalised Banks to cater to the needs of the elite and the money bags only. The Committee has favoured entry of foreign banks and has recommended liberalisation ol licensing policy by RBI. In the name of the capital adequacy, the Committee wants the banks to approach "capital market, so that eventually the banks will be captives of the vested interests. In blind emulation of the developed countries, the Committee has recommended norms for recognition of income and classification of assets which when implemented will paint a weird but untrue picture of Indian Banking. In cover-up of politically induced bad advances, only the committee has recommended setting up of an Asset Reconstruction Fund to absorb all the bad and doubtful debts of the Banks. The Committee has glossed over the real problems of the banking industry namely restructuring, reforms of administrative systems, revision of archaic procedures, man-power, motivation, management styles, need for MOUs as against continuous interference by Government, etc.

The Council unanimously rejects the recommendations of the Narasimham Committee and calls upon the working class to trust-rate by collective action the subtle moves of the Government to denationalize the banks.

Annexure 7: Resolution on the New Economic Policies passed by the third General Council of the AIBOC.

On the New Economic Policies

The All India Bank Officers' Confederation meeting in its 3rd Triennial Session at Agra on 16th, 17th & 18th December 1992 after in-depth consideration, is of the view that the New Economic Policies and the so called reforms initiated by the Government would only lead to widening of the disparities in wealth and income and further impoverish the masses of the country. The policies tend to negate the concept of a Welfare State. In a country beset with poverty and unemployment, the State has to be the guardian angel of the poor and the deprived. The teeming millions cannot be left to fend for themselves and to survive against the oppressive forces of monopolists and profiteers. The State has to step in with controls and other mechanism to maintain the balance and to ensure that fruits of labour are equitably distributed and that the economic activity is geared to balanced regional development The Council feds that the policies of the Government amount to surrender of the nation's sell respect and sovereignty to the World Bank and the IME By these policies the country would slide back to the era of colonization (without physical occupation) There can be no purposeful economic or political independence if all the vital sectors of the economy are eventually controlled by multinationals, which is the logical conclusion of the World Bank and IMF conditional ties.

The General Council calls upon all the sections of the Indian people to study the implications of the experience of other countries that have suffered as a result of the IMF forced structural adjustments and to launch a struggle in the nature of the freedom movement to safeguard the economic and political independence of the motherland. The Council directs that all steps be taken to resist the policies of the Government of India and the onslaught of the World Bank and IMF working in unison.

Bibliography

Primary Sources

1. Articles from common bond

"Agitation Creates Impact—Government Holds Talks with AIBOC," *Common Bond,* February 1986, 6.

"AIBOC Activists' Meeting at Bhubaneswar." *Common Bond,* July 1986, 7.

"AIBOC Activities in Full Swing." *Common Bond,* November 1985, 4.

"AIBOC Sphere Widens—Majority Achieved in Private Sector." *Common Bond,* August 1987, 6.

"AIBOC Wins Case in Supreme Court." *Common Bond,* September 1989, 4.

"AIPSBOF." *Common Bond,* May 1989, 6.

"All India Bank Officers' Confederation—8th Triennial General Council," *Common Bond,* April 2008, 1-32.

"All India Co-operative Sector Banks' Officers' Federation." *Common Bond,* May 1989, 4.

"Co-ordination Committee Meets at Delhi." *Common Bond,* December 1987, 1.

"First Conference of the State Unit." *Common Bond,* June 1986, 6.

"Inauguration of Goa Unit." *Common Bond,* May 1986, 7.

"Karnataka State Unit Launched." *Common Bond,* May 1986, 7.

"Maharashtra Unit - State Conference." *Common Bond,* May 1986, 5.

"Mobilization in Full Swing." *Common Bond,* April 1987, 1.

"New Affiliates of AIBOC." *Common Bond,* June 1986, 2.

"Office-bearers Elected." *Common Bond,* August 1986, 7.

"Premature Retirements—I.B.A's Version," *Common Bond,* February 1986, 7.

"R.R.B. Officers." *Common Bond,* November 1986, 7.

"Regional Rural Banks' Officers - Revision of Terms and Conditions of Service." *Common Bond,* August 1987, 1-2.

"Report from Bihar Unit." *Common Bond,* July 1986, 6.

"Seminar on Women in Banking." *Common Bond,* January 1996, 1.

"Service Condition of R.R.B. Officers." *Common Bond,* February 1987, 8.

"Setting up of a Federation for Officers of Private Sector Banks." *Common Bond,* February 1987, 4.

"State Bank Group - Salary Revision." *Common Bond,* May 1986.

"Well Done Mr. Chari." *Common Bond,* February 1987, 5.

"AIBOC Executive Committee Meets at Calcutta," *Common Bond,* April 2000, 2.

"Fight against Privatisation to Continue," *Common Bond,* October 1991, 3.

"Government Releases Rs. 400 Crores Capital to UCO, UBI and Indian Bank," *Common Bond,* April 1999, 15.

"Joint Action against the Move for Privatisation of Banks - Strike on 6th September 1991," *Common Bond,* September 1991, 1.

"Joint Struggle Committee of Financial Sector Union," *Common Bond,* December 1999, 5-7.

"Memorandum Submitted to the Finance Minister," *Common Bond,* November 1991, 7-10.

"Morcha to LIC at Pondicherry," *Common Bond,* January 2000, 9.

"Privatisation Bill Introduced in Parliament," *Common Bond,* December 2000, 1.

"Regulation 20(1) Strikes Again," *Common Bond,* May 1986, 4.

"Tackling the Problem of Weak Banks," *Common Bond,* April 1999, 10-11.

"UCO, UBI Emit Revival Sparks," *Common Bond,* August 2000, 6.

"UFBU Appears Before Narasimham Committee," *Common Bond,* April 1998, 1-8.

"UFBU Delegation Meets RBI Governor," *Common Bond,* December 1999, 2-4.

"UFBU Meets Unions in UBI, UCO and India Bank," *Common Bond,* May 1999, 1-2.

"UFBU Meets Verma Committee," *Common Bond,* June 1999, 4-6.

"Verma Committee Report – Categorisation of Public Sector Banks," *Common Bond,* November 1999, 4.

"Verma's Explosion," *Common Bond,* November 1999, 1-3.

"Workshop on Narasimham Committee Report," *Common Bond,* March 1992, 11.

Godbole, R.N. ed., "Undeclared Emergency Grips Banks," *Common Bond,* January 1986, 1.

Godbole, R.N., ed. "AICOBOO Revives Its Charter of Demands." *Common Bond,* June 1982, 4.

Godbole, R.N., ed. "Gearing up the Organisational Machine." *Common Bond,* June 1985, 1-2.

Godbole, R.N., ed. "Salary Revision Finalised." *Common Bond,* October 1985.

Godbole, R.N., ed. "Salary Revision." *Common Bond,* May 1985, 1-2.

Godbole, R.N., ed. "Standardisation Scheme for Six Banks." *Common Bond,* July 1982, 3.

Godbole, R.N., ed. "Token Strike on 13 August." *Common Bond,* August 1985, 1-2.

Sengupta, S.R. "Emergence of AIBOC - Logic Was Inexorable." *Common Bond,* December 1985, 1-9.

2. Circulars

AIBOC, AIBOA, INBOC, and NOBO. *Charter of Demands Submitted to IBA on 2 May 2017.* PDF. March 29, 2018.

Godbole, R.N. *Agitation by Officers of UCO Bank – Fraternal Support,* Circular No. 26 (Bangalore, Karnataka: All India Bank Officers' Confederation (AIBOC), 1988), 1.

Godbole, R.N. *AIPSBOF Launched.* Circular No. 22. Bangalore, Karnataka: All India Bank Officers' Confederation (AIBOC), 1988.

Godbole, R.N. *Andhra Bank Officers Free Themselves.* Circular No. 28. Bangalore, Karnataka: All India Bank Officers' Confederation (AIBOC), 1989.

Godbole, R.N. *Bank Officers' Movement Takes Off.* Circular No. 1. Bangalore, Karnataka: All India Bank Officers' Confederation (AIBOC), 1985.

Godbole, R.N. *Committees of AIBOC.* Circular No. 7. Bangalore, Karnataka: All India Bank Officers' Confederation (AIBOC), 1985. 1-5.

Godbole, R.N. *New Star on the Horizon*. Circular No. 29. Bangalore, Karnataka: All India Bank Officers' Confederation (AIBOC), 1989.

Godbole, R.N. *Revision of Salary Structure of Private Sector Banks Officers*. Circular No. 8. Bangalore, Karnataka: All India Bank Officers' Confederation (AIBOC), 1985. 1-2.

Godbole, R.N. *State Units Fund*. Circular No. 13. Bangalore, Karnataka: All India Bank Officers' Confederation (AIBOC), 1985.

Rishabadas, D.S. *10th Bipartite – Road Blocks in the Negotiations AIBOC Is Fully Prepared to Overcome*. Circular No. 21. Bangalore, Karnataka: All India Bank Officers' Confederation (AIBOC), 2013.

Rishabadas, D.S. *10th Bipartite Meeting Scheduled for 4 March, 2013; Postponed*. Circular No. 12. Bangalore, Karnataka: All India Bank Officers' Confederation (AIBOC), 2013.

Rishabadas, D.S. *Submission of Charter of Demands—10th Bipartite Negotiations to Commence*. Circular No. 82. Bangalore, Karnataka: All India Bank Officers' Confederation (AIBOC), 2012.

Rishabadas, D.S. *UFBU Circular No. 5 Dated 22 February, 2013*. Circular No. 11. Bangalore, Karnataka: All India Bank Officers' Confederation (AIBOC), 2013.

Singh, Harvinder. *A Long Drawn Battle Concludes – 10th Bipartite Settlement Signed*. Circular No. 25. Bangalore, Karnataka: All India Bank Officers' Confederation (AIBOC), 2015.

3. The proceedings of the General Councils

Amendments to Bye-laws. Bangalore, Karnataka: All India Bank Officers' Confederation (AIBOC), 1993. 1-16.

Constitution of the AIBOC (As Amended up to 10 March, 2008). Bangalore, Karnataka: All India Bank Officers' Confederation (AIBOC), 2008.

Godbole, R.N. "Report of the General Secretary to the 1st Session of General Council." *Common Bond*, January 1987, 1-22.

Godbole, R.N. "Report of the General Secretary to the 2nd Session of General Council." *Common Bond*, January 1990, 1-37.

Godbole, R.N. "Report of the General Secretary to the 4th Session of General Council." *Common Bond*, July 1995, 1-29.

Godbole, R.N. *Report of the General Secretary to the 3rd Session of General Council*. Bangalore, Karnataka: All India Bank Officers' Confederation (AIBOC), 1992. 59-90.

Godbole, R.N, *Report of the General Secretary to the 11th Annual Conference of All India State Bank of India Officers' Federation*, 1977.

Godbole, R.N, *Report of the General Secretary to the 13th Annual Conference of All India State Bank of India Officers' Federation*, 1980.

Godbole, R.N. *Report of the General Secretary to the 10th Annual Conference of All India State Bank of India Supervising Staff Federation*, 1975.

Sen Gupta, S.R. "Report of the General Secretary to the 5th Session of General Council," *Common Bond*, January 1999, 1- 33.

Secondary Sources

1. Books and articles

All India Bank Officer' Confederation. *AIBOC—IBA Joint Notes on Wage Revisions*. Bangalore: All India Bank Officer' Confederation, 2010.

Bagchi, Amiya Kumar. *The Evolution of the State Bank of India*. Bombay: Oxford University Press, 1987.

Bal, Shanti R. et al., *History of Bank Employees Movement*. West Bengal: Bank Employees Federation of India Publication, 2015.

Braverman, Harry. *Labor and Monopoly Capital; the Degradation of Work in the Twentieth Century*. New York: Monthly Review Press, 1974.

Challenges and Strategies 1985-2010. Bangalore, Karnataka: All India Bank Officers' Confederation (AIBOC), 2011.

Chandrasekhar, C.P., and Jayati Ghosh. *Indian Banking - Current Challenges and Alternatives for the Future*. New Delhi: Economic Research Foundation, 2018.

Dev, D.T. Franco Rajendra. *Glimpses of the Historic Indefinite Strike 1969*. Bangalore: All India State Bank of India Officers Federation, 2009.

Ghosh, Jayati, C.P. Chandrasekhar, and Prabhat Patnaik. *Demonetisation Decoded A Critique of Indias Currency Experiment*. Milton: Taylor and Francis, 2017.

Ghosh, P.K. "Structure of Trade Union Organisation." *The Economic Weekly*, March 27, 1965, 562-65.

Kanhere, Usha S. *Managerial Trade Unionism: A Sociological Study of Officers Association in Nationalized Banks in Ahmedabad*. Delhi, India: Mittal Publications, 1987.

Kumar, Virenda. "Committee for Standardization of Pay Scales,

Allowances and Perquisites of Officers in the Nationalised Banks, 1973." In *Committees and Commissions in India*, 228-33. Vol. XI. New Delhi: Concept, 1994.

Lenin, V.I, *Imperialism: The Highest Stage of Capitalism (1917)*, Leftword Books, 2000 Reprint.

Panandikar, S.G., and D.M. Mithani. *Banking in India*. Bombay: Orient Longman, 1975.

Revri, Chamanlal. *The Indian Trade Union Movement: An Outline History 1880-1947*. New Delhi: Orient Longman, 1972.

Saez, Lawrence. *Banking reform in India and China*. Springer, 2004.

Sen, Sukomal. *Working class of India: history of Emergence and Movement, 1830-1970*. K.P. Bagchi, 1977.

Sengupta, S.R. *Bank Officers' Movement; Perspective and Journey*. Kolkata: Foundation for United Trade Union Research & Education (FUTURE), 2010.

2. Theses

Rosaiah, T. "Human Resource Management in Commercial Banks." PhD thesis, Sri Krishnadevaraya University, 1994.

3. Interviews

A.K. Jana (Former President of AIBOC), interviewed by Sarika Chaudhary, Bangalore, India, November 2017.

D.T. Franco (Current Secretary General of AIBOC), interviewed by Sarika Chaudhary, Bangalore, India, May 2018.

G.D. Nadaf (Former General Secretary of AIBOC), interviewed by Sarika Chaudhary, Bangalore, India, February 2018.

Harvinder Singh (Former General Secretary of AIBOC), interviewed by Sarika Chaudhary, Bangalore, India, June 2018.

K.V. Acharya (Current President of AIBPARC), interviewed by Sarika Chaudhary, New Delhi, India, November 2017.

L.V. Subramaniam (Former Secretary General of AICOBOO), interviewed by Sarika Chaudhary, Bangalore, India, February 2018.

Shantha Raju (Former General Secretary of the AIBOC), interviewed by Sarika Chaudhary, Bangalore, India, February 2018.

Y. Sundershan (Former President of AIBOC), interviewed by Sarika Chaudhary, Bangalore, India, June 2018.

Joint Notes on Wage Revisions between AIBOC and IBA

IVth Bipartite Settlement

Salary Revision for Bank Officers

With effect from: 1.2.1984 Date of Joint Note: 24.9.1985

Signatories on behalf of IBA	On behalf of officers' assns.
1. M.N. Goiporia	1. R.N. Godbole
2. R. Srinivasan	2. S.R. Sen Gupta
3. L.B. Bhide	3. R.C. Agarwal
4. N.S. Pradhan	4. M.U. Pai
5. B.D. Upasani	5. V.B. Naik
6. S.A. Farooqi	6. K.N. Kannan
7. A.K. Bakshy	
8. V.S. Kamat Khadpe	

Salary Revision Finalised

w.e.f. from 01-02-1984

We are happy to inform members that the deadlock over the date of effect for salary revision proposals has at last been resolved. After discussions on 9th & 13th September and again on 23rd and 24th September, an agreement has finally been reached with the Indian Banks' Association.

Members are aware, that the Government made sweeping changes in the earlier proposals by arbitrarily shifting the date of effect to 1st July 1984. This led to a strong sense of resentment amongst all the Officers in the Banking Industry, culminating in a day's token strike on the 13th August 1985.

Sensing the strong resentment of Officers the Government reviewed the matter, and thanks to the timely intervention of Hon'ble Finance Minister, Shri V. P. Singh, talks were resumed without any further loss of time. The talks were held in a cordial climate culminating in an agreement on the 24th September 1985, conceding retrospective effect w.e. f. 1st February 1984.

Scales of Pay: While there has been no change in the IBA's earlier offer relating to Basic Pay & Dearness Allowance, members would be getting a slightly higher quantum by way of House Rent Allowance. The categorisation norms have also been suitably revised, due to our strong opposition to the earlier formula as suggested by the Government.

Our congratulations to members for their solid support and for having responded to our calls with rock-like solidarity, projecting an image of unity and exemplary organisational discipline. It is due to the implicit faith of members at alt levels that we were able to clinch the deal and strike a better bargain. The historic strike of 13th August 1985 moved the Government to give up their uncompromising and rigid attitude, seeing the determination of the Officers to fight out the injustices, whatever may be the sacrifices on their part.

Anyway, the long awaited salary revision is at last over. But the curtain is not fully drawn as there are a lot of connected issues yet to be sorted out with the I.B.A. Discussions on miscellaneous issues are to commence soon. The struggles ensure parity to Private Sector Banks will also begin.

Vth Bipartite Settlement

Indian Banks' Association

Personnel Department

Stadium House Block 3
Veer Nariman Road,
Bombay-400020.
Phone Office: 222365
Grams 'BANKSLINK' Telex No. 011-5146

No. PD/OSR/8 October 18, 1989

Chief Executives of all the
Nationalised Banks.
Dear Sirs,

Salary Revision for Officer Employees—Amendments to Officers' service Regulations

Further to our circular No. PD/OSR/2 dated 12th June, 1989, we have to advise that the Government have since conveyed approval to the draft amendments to the Officers' Service Regulations, 1979/1982 as proposed by the IBA, for carrying out the salary revision. A copy of the draft amendments to be made in the Officers' Service Regulations, 1979/1982 as approved by the Government is enclosed for your necessary action. We also enclose a copy of the communication dated 13th October, 1989 conveying Government's approval for your information. The Regulations in the existing form together with the proposed amendments are indicated for reference only.

You may kindly initiate the process for the amendments to Regulation 3, 4, 5, 21, 22, 23, 24, 25, 34, 41, 42, 45 and 46 of the Officers' Service Regulations as par the draft amendments enclosed, in terms of Section 19(1) of the Banking Companies (Acquisition and Transfer of Undertakings) Act, 1970/1980.

The implementation of Regulations 17, 23, 24 and 34 will be subject to the vacation of the stay granted by the Andhra

Pradesh High Court in writ Petition No. 11809 of. 1989 filed by the All India Bank Officers' Association. We are taking necessary steps for vacating the stay. We shall keep you informed in this regard.

Yours faithfully,

(A.K. Bakshy)
Secretary

cc. to

1) Designated Officers
2) State Bank of India and its Associate Banks
3) Government of India, Ministry of Finance, Department of Economic Affairs (Banking Division), New Delhi.
4) Chief Officer, Reserve Bank of India, Central Office, Department of Banking Operation & Development, Bombay.

M.N. Buch
Joint Secretary
(Tel. No. 352478)

Ministry of Finance
Department of Economic Affairs
(Banking Division) "Jeevan Deep"
Parliament Street:
New Delhi-110001

D.O. F. No. 1/1/21/87-IR

Dated : 13th October 1989

Deer Shri Srinivasan,

Please refer to your letter No. PD/HNS/85/665/1094 dated 11 th September 1989 regarding proposed amendments to the Officers' Service Regulation following the salary revision of officer employees. We have examined the draft amendments to the OSRs enclosed to your letter under reference. We are in agreement with the proposed amendments except that the clause '(iv) All other places' appearing in proposed Regulation 22(2) may be replaced by clause '(iv) Area III.'

You are requested to please circulate the drafts 'among the nationalised banks immediately for appropriate action in terms Section 19(1) of the Banking Companies (Acquisition & Transfer of Undertakings) Act, 1970/80.

A copy of the final draft circulated among the banks may be endorsed to us as well as to RBI.

The proposed guidelines enclosed with your letter under reference are being examined and would be issued separately.

With regards,

Shri R. Srinivasan, Chairman,
Indian Banks' Association,
Bomaby.

VIth Bipartite Settlement

Salary Revision for Officers

Conclusion of Discussions Between the IBA and The Officers' Organisations

The IBA's High Power Committee for Discussions with Officers' Organisations held several rounds of discussions with the representatives of the Officers' Organisations on the salary revision for officers in public sector banks. During these discussions common views have emerged between the two sides. The outcome of such discussions acceptable to both sides is given in the Annexure-I.

The representatives of the officers' organisations stated that the outcome of the discussions as given in the Annexure-I was in full satisfaction of their demands raised during the discussions in this regard and the existing service conditions be modified to that extent. The residual issues shall be taken up for discussions as early as possible.

The IBA agrees that it shall recommend to the public sector banks to initiate the process to amend the Officers' Service Regulations, to give effect to what is stated in the Annexure-I. The IBA shall also recommend to the Government of India to approve the amendments and to issue appropriate guidelines necessary for this purpose.

The IBA shall also recommend to the private sector banks which are 'A class banks (listed in the Annexure-ll) and which have authorised the IBA in this regard to effect the salary revision for their officers upto Scale III on the same lines as given in the Annexure-I.

The IBA desired substantial enhancement in the existing norms for categorisation of branches considering that the last revision was done 10 years ago. After discussions it has been agreed that the revised norms could be as given in the Annexure, w.e.f. May, 1995.

The representatives of officers' organisations have suggested that pending formal amendments to the Officers' Service Regulations as per procedure laid down under Section

19(1) of the Banking Companies (Acquisition and Transfer of Undertakings) Act, 1970/1980, the IBA may advise the banks to disburse immediately an ad hoc amount, equivalent to the net arrears payable for the period November, 1992 to June- 1995 and continue to pay revised salary and allowances on ad hoc basis. The IBA has agreed to make appropriate 'recommendations to the Government in this regard for its consideration.

Representatives of the officers' organisations assured, full cooperation will be extended by them, their affiliates and members, in measures, aimed at improving customer service, development and expansion of banking and maintenance of healthy and harmonious industrial relations in the banking industry.

For Indian Banks' Association	For All India Bank Officers' Confederation (S/Shri)
Rashid Jilani	S.R. Sen Gupta
S.K. Soni	Umed Singh
A.T. Panner Selvam	R.N. Godbole
S. Srinivasan	K.D. Khera
A.K. Bakhshy	R.C. Agarwal
K.V. Krishnamurthy	P.V. Mathew

23.6.1995

VIIth Bipartite Settlement

Salary Revision For Officers

Conclusion of Discussions between the IBA and the Officers' Associations

The Negotiating Committee of IBA representing the management in the ongoing negotiations with officers' associations held several rounds of discussions with the representatives of the officers' associations on salary revision for officers in Public Sector Banks (Annexure II). In the course of the deliberations common view points have emerged between the two parties. The fruitful outcome of the discussions acceptable to both sides Is enlisted in Annexure I to this Note.

The representatives of the officers' associations have expressed satisfaction at the outcome of the negotiations as stated in Annexure" I. The representatives have also agreed that the, existing service conditions be modified in conformity with what has been stated in Annexure I.

The IBA agreed that it shall recommend to the Public Sector Banks to initiate the process of amending the.Officers' Service Regulations and Bank Employees' Pension. Regulations, 1995, in orderto implement what is stated in Annexure I. The IBA shall also recommend to the Government of India to approve the amendments and to issue appropriate guidelines necessary for this purpose. The IBA shall take steps, to recommend to the Private Sector Banks which are 'A class banks (listed in Annexure III) and which have authorised the IBA in this regard, to give effect to the salary revision for their officers upto Scale III on the same lines as given In Annexure I.

The representatives of officers' associations have requested that pending for al amendments to the Officers' Service Regulations as per procedure laid down under Section 19(1) of the Banking Companies (Acquisition and Transfer of Undertakings) Act, 1970/1980, the IBA may advise the banks to disburse Immediately an adhoc amount, equivalent to the net arrears payable for the period April 1998 to November 1999 and continue to pay revised salary and allowances on adhoc basis. The IBA has agreed to make suitable recommendations to the Government In' this regard for its consideration.

The Officer's Association demanded one more option for pension considering the fact that many could not earlier of the "Strike Clause". IBA, however, expressed its inability to consider the demand.

Representatives of the officers' associations have assured full cooperation on their part, their affiliates and members, in implementation of measures aimed at improving customer service, optimum utilisation of manpower, expansion of barrking activities to take on the competition and challenges confronting the industry and maintenance of healthy and harmonious industrial relations in the banking industry.

December 14, 1999.

For Indian Banks' Association	For All India Bank Officers' Confederation (S/Shri)
A.T. Pannir Selvam	1) Shantha Raju
Harbhajan Singh	2) S.R. Sen Gupta
Dalbir Singh	3) R.C. Agarwal
S. Rajagopal	4) K.D. Khera
Y. Radhakrishnan	5) M Balakrishna
K.M. Mehrotra	6) P.V. Mathew

A.D. Navaneethan

M.N. Dandekar

Yogesh Chandra

Allen C.A. Pereira

7) S. Roy Chowdhury

8) A. Ananthakrishna Rao

For All India Bank Offiers' Association (S/Shri)

1) Debesh Bhattacharjee

2) R.J. Sridharan

3) Alok Khare

4) Sunil K. Srivastava

For Indian National Bank Offiers' Congress

1) K.K. Nair

2) S. Ganeshan

3) Shanthakumar

4) M.M. Bhaskara Rao

For National Organisation of Bank Offiers (S/Shri)

1) S.N. Joshi

2) Ashok Pandey

3) D.R. Shirodkar

4) S.K. Rathod

VIIIth Bipartite Settlement

Salary Revision for Officers

Conclusion of Discussions between the IBA and the Officers' Associations

The Negotiating Committee of IBA representing the managements of Banks held several rounds of discussions with the authorised representatives of the Officers' Associations on salary revision for officers in Banks. In the course of the deliberations, common view points have emerged between the two parties. The outcome of the discussions acceptable to both sides is listed in Annexure I to this Note. The representatives of the officers' associations have also agreed that the existing service conditions be modified to the extent what has been stated in Annexure-I.

IBA agreed that it shall recommend to the Public Sector Banks, as in Annexure-II, to initiate the process of amending the Officers' Service Regulations and Bank Employees' Pension Regulations, 1995, in order to implement what is stated in Annexure-I. The IBA shall also recommend to the Government of India to approve the amendments and to issue appropriate guidelines necessary for this purpose.

IBA shall take steps to recommend to the Private Sector Banks which are listed in Annexure-III and which have authorized the IBA in this regard, to give effect to the salary revision for their officers upto Scale-III on the same lines as mentioned in Annexure-I.

The representatives of Officers' Associations have requested that pending formal amendments to the Officers' Service Regulations as per procedure laid down under Section 19(1) of the Banking Companies (Acquisition and Transfer of Undertakings) Act, 1970/1980, IBA may advise the banks to disburse immediately an ad-hoc amount, equivalent to the net arrears payable for the period 1-11-2002 to 31-5-2005 and continue to pay revised salary and allowances on ad-hoc basis. IBA has agreed to make suitable recommendations to the Government in this regard for its consideration.

The Officers' Associations demanded one more option for pension considering the fact that many could not opt earlier for various reasons. IBA, however, reiterated its inability to extend the present pension scheme to those who had not opted for pension. However, both the parties agreed to discuss alternative proposals.

The Officers' associations on behalf of the officer-employees in banks listed in Annexure II & III agree that the understandings reached as detailed in Annexure-I hereto are in full satisfaction of their demands.

Representatives of the Officers' Associations have assured full co-operation on their part, their affiliates and members, in implementation of measures aimed at improving customer service, optimum utilisation of manpower, expansion of banking activities to take on the competition and challenges confronting the industry and maintenance of healthy and harmonious industrial relations in the banking industry.

Dated 2nd June 2005.

For Indian Banks' Association (S/Shri)

1) A.K. Purwar

2) Dr. Dalbir Singh

3) V.P. Shetty

4) S.C. Basu

5) M.S. Kapur

For All India Bank Officers' Confederation (S/Shri)

1) R.C. Agarwal

2) Shantha Raju

3) K.V. Acharya

4) T.R. Bhat

5) Amar Pal

6) M.B.N. Rao

7) Dr. A.K. Khandelwal

8) Anantha Krishna

9) A. Datta

10) S.A. Farooqi

11) A.C. Verma

12) H.N. Sinor

13) R. Srivasankara Babu

14) G. Sankaranarayanan

6) P.J. Shah

7) P.V. Mathew

8) P.K. Sarkar

9) V. Eswaran

10) S.K. Shetty

For All India Bank Offiers' Association (S/Shri)

1) Alok Khare

For National Organisation of Bank Offiers (S/Shri)

1) S.V. Joshi

2) Sunil K. Srivastava

3) R.J. Sridharan

4) S. Nagarajan

2) S.N. Joshi

3) S.K. Rathod

4) B.K. Irwarthraya

For Indian National Bank Offiers' Congress (S/Shri)

1) Shanthakumar

2) T.K. Balasubramanian

3) M.M. Bhaskara Rao

4) Subash Choudhry

IXth Bipartite Settlement

Salary Revision for Officers

Conclusion of Discussions between the IBA and the Officers' Associations

1. The Negotiating Committee of Indian Banks' Association (IBA) representing the managements of banks held several rounds of discussions with the authorised representatives of the Officers' Associations on salary revision and other issues concerning service conditions for officers in Banks. In the course of the deliberations, common viewpoints have emerged between the two parties. The outcome of the discussions acceptable to both sides is listed in Annexure I to this Note. The representatives of the Officers' Associations have also agreed that the existing service conditions be modified to the extent what has been stated in Annexure I.
2. The representatives of the Officers' Associations, a part of United Forum of Bank Unions (UFBU) and IBA entered into a Memorandum of Understanding on 25th February 2008 on various issues. Extending another option for pension to those who did not opt for pension when Bank Employees' Pension Regulations, 1995 dated 29th September 1995/26th March 1996 were implemented was one of the issues to be considered. After several rounds of discussions and valuing the liability through an actuarial calculation, it is agreed to extend another option to join the pension scheme to those who did not opt for pension when Bank Employees' Pension Regulations, 1995 dated 29th September 1995/ 26th March 1996 were implemented, on the terms and conditions agreed and incorporated in the Joint Note dated 27th April 2010 signed between the parties.
3. IBA agreed that it shall recommend to the Public Sector Banks, as in Annexure II, to initiate the process of amending the Officers' Service Regulations and Bank Employees' Pension Regulations, 1995 dated

29th September 1995/ 26th March 1996, in order to implement what is stated in Annexure I. The IBA shall also recommend to the Government of India to approve the amendments and to issue appropriate guidelines necessary for this purpose.

4. IBA shall take steps to recommend to the Private Sector Banks which are listed in Annexure III and which have authorised the IBA in this regard, to give effect to the salary revision for their officers upto Scale III on the same lines as mentioned in Annexure I.
5. The representatives of Officers' Associations have requested that pending formal amendments to the Officers' Service Regulations as per procedure laid down under Section 19(1) of the Banking Companies (Acquisition and Transfer of Undertakings) Act, 1970/1980, IBA may advise the banks to disburse immediately an ad-hoc amount, equivalent to the net arrears payable for the period from 1 st November 2007 to 30th April 2010 and continue to pay revised salary and allowances on ad-hoc basis. IBA has agreed to make suitable recommendations to the Government in this regard for its consideration.
6. The Officers' Associations on behalf of the officer-employees in banks listed in Annexures II & III agree that the understandings reached as detailed in Annexure I hereto are in full satisfaction of their demands.
7. Management proposed that a scheme for introduction of performance linked variable pay in addition to fixed pay be considered as part of this wage revision exercise to increase efficiency in operations. After preliminary discussions, it was decided to pursue the matter further.
8. Representatives of the Officers' Associations have assured full co-operation on their part, their affiliates and members, in implementation of measures aimed at improving customer service, optimum utilisation of manpower, expansion of banking activities to take on the competition and challenges confronting the industry and maintenance of healthy and harmonious industrial relations in the banking industry.

Mumbai

Dated : 27th April 2010

For Indian Banks' Association (S/Shri)

M.V. Nair

R. Sridharan

Narayanan Raja

K. Ramakrishnan

Rajeeve Rishi

B.B. Das

K. Unnikrishnan

M. Venugopalan

For All India Bank Officers' Confederation (S/Shri)

K.S. Shetty

G.D. Nadaf

P.V. Mathew

P.K. Sarkar

T.T. Natarajan

K. Ananda Kumar

T.N. Goel

S.K. Kohli

K. Ramakoteswara Rao

G. Muthuswamy

K.D. Kheda

X^{th} Bipartite Settlement

Salary Revision for Officers

Conclusion of Discussion between the IBA and the Officers' Associations

The Negotiating Committee of Indian Banks' Association (IBA) representing the managements of banks held several rounds of discussions with the authorised representatives of the Officers' Associations an salary revision and other issues concerning service conditions far officers in Banks. In the course of the deliberations, common viewpoints have emerged between the two parties. The outcome of the discussions acceptable to both sides is listed in Annexure I to this Nate. The representatives of the Officers' Associations have also agreed that the existing service conditions be modified to the extent what has been stated in Annexure I.

2. IBA agreed that it shall recommend to the Public Sector Banks, as in Annexure II, to initiate the process of amending the Officers' Service Regulations and Bank Employees' Pension Regulations, 1995 dated 29th September 1995/ 26th March 1996, in order to implement what is stated in Annexure I. The IBA shall also recommend to the Government of India to approve the amendments and to issue appropriate guidelines necessary far this purpose.
3. IBA shall take steps to recommend to the Private Sector Banks which are listed in Annexure Ill and which have authorised the IBA in this regard, to give effect to the salary revision far their officers upto Scale Ill an the same lines as mentioned in Annexure I.
4. The representatives of Officers' Associations have requested that pending formal amendments to the Officers' Service Regulations/Rules as per procedure laid dawn under Section 19(1) of the Banking Companies (Acquisition and Transfer of Undertakings) Act, 1970/1980 and the applicable provision of State Bank of India Act, 1955. IBA may advise the banks to disburse immediately

an ad-hac amount, equivalent to the net arrears payable far the period from 1st November 2012 to 31st May 2015 and continue to pay revised salary and allowances an ad-hac basis. IBA has agreed to make suitable recommendations to the Government in this regard far its consideration.

5. The Officers' Associations on behalf of the officer-employees In banks listed In Annexures II & III agree that the understandings reached as detailed in Annexure I here to are in full satisfaction of their demands.
6. IBA reiterated and made presentation of a scheme for introduction of performance linked variable pay in addition to fixed pay be considered as part of this wage revision exercise to increase efficiency in operations. After discussions, it was decided to pursue the matter at a later stage.
7. Representatives of the Officers' Associations have assured full co-operation on their part,their affiliates and members, in implementation of measures aimed at improving customer service, optimum utilisation of manpower, expansion of banking activities to take on the competition and challenges confronting the industry and maintenance of healthy and harmonious industrial relations in the banking industry.

Place: Mumbai

Dated: 25th May 2015

For Indian Banks' Association (S/Shri)	For All India Bank Officers' Confederation (S/Shri)
T.M. Bhasin	Y. Sudarshan
Ashwani Kumar	Harvinder Singh

Animesh Chauhan

Shyam Srinivasan

Ashwini Mehra

M.V. Tanksale

K. Unnikrishnan

K.S. Chauhan

K. Ananda Kumar

G.V. Manimaran

Dilip Saha

V. Raghavendra Sarma

Harshvardhan M.

P.V. Mohanan

D.N. Prakash

Thomas Franco

Debasis Ghosh

Sanjay A. Manjrekar

K. Rajendran

M. Sreenath

Sunil Kumar

For All India Bank Officers' Association

Alok Khare	S.S. Shishodia
Dr. Kumar Arvind	S. Nagarajan
M.A. Srinivasan	S.N. Dutta
Shri G. Gunasekaran	Narendra Kotiawala

For Indian National Bank Officers Congress

K.K. Nair	V.V. Ramana
Dr. R. Chandramoorthy	R.C. Sharma
Ajit Kumar Ghosh	Nagesh D. Dande

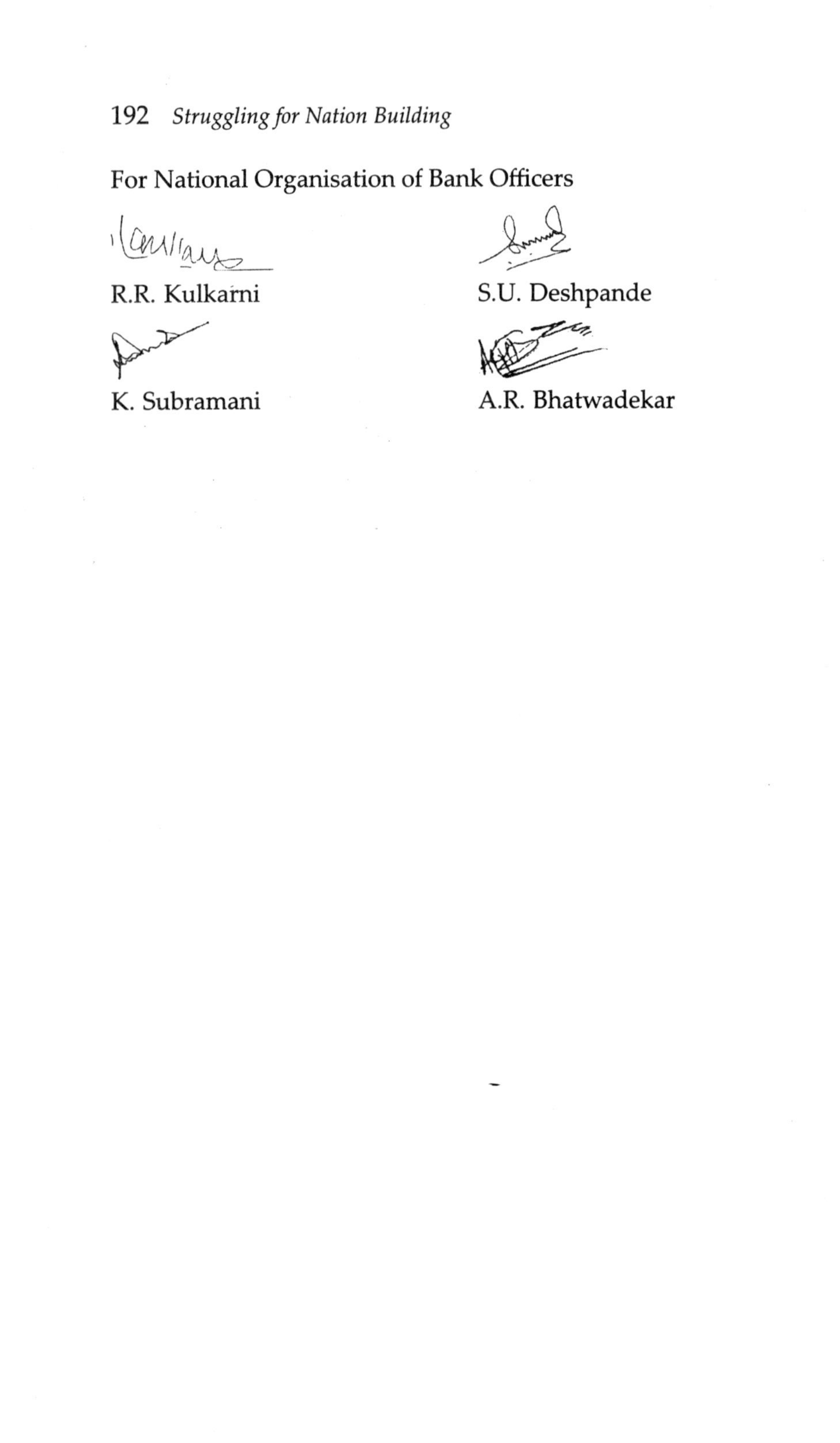

For National Organisation of Bank Officers

R.R. Kulkarni	S.U. Deshpande
K. Subramani	A.R. Bhatwadekar

Other Important AIBOC Publications

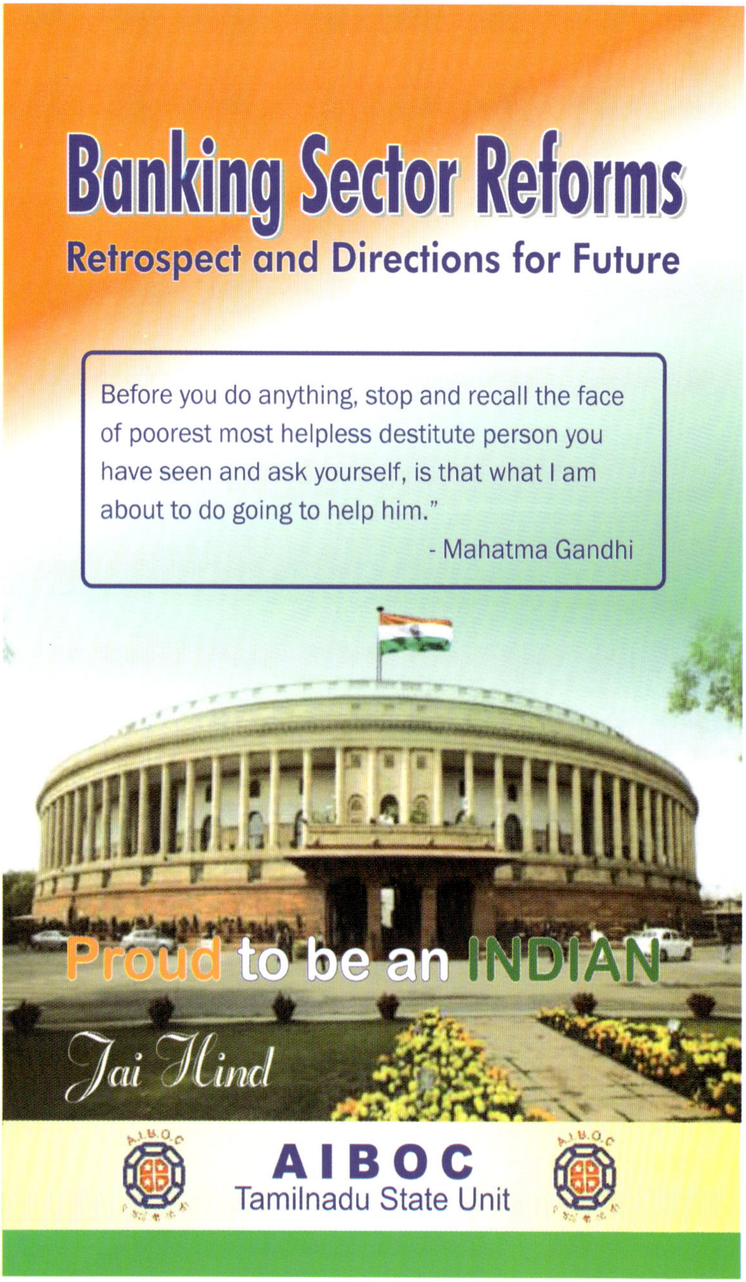
Banking Sector Reforms
Retrospect and Directions for Future
Before you do anything, stop and recall the face of poorest most helpless destitute person you have seen and ask yourself, is that what I am about to do going to help him."
- Mahatma Gandhi
Proud to be an INDIAN
Jai Hind
AIBOC
Tamilnadu State Unit

CHARTER OF DEMANDS SUBMITTED BY

ALL INDIA BANK OFFICERS' CONFEDERATION [AIBOC]
ALL INDIA BANK OFFICERS' ASSOCIATION [AIBOA]
INDIAN NATIONAL BANK OFFICERS' CONGRESS [INBOC]
NATIONAL ORGANISATION OF BANK OFFICERS [NOBO]

TO

INDIAN BANK ASSOCIATION MUMBAI
ON 2ND MAY 2017

The Basic principle of our wage revision should be based on the Constitution of India which begins as,
"WE, THE PEOPLE OF INDIA, having solemnly resolved to constitute India into a SOVEREIGN SOCIALIST SECULAR DEMOCRATIC REPUBLIC and to secure to all its citizens: JUSTICE, SOCIAL, ECONOMIC AND POLITICAL; LIBERTY of thought, expression, belief, faith and worship; EQUALITY of status and of opportunity; and to promote among them all FRATERNITY assuring the dignity of the individual and the unity and integrity of the Nation; IN OUR CONSTITUENT ASSEMBLY this twenty-sixth day of November, 1949, do HEREBY ADOPT, ENACT AND GIVE TO OURSELVES THIS CONSTITUTION."

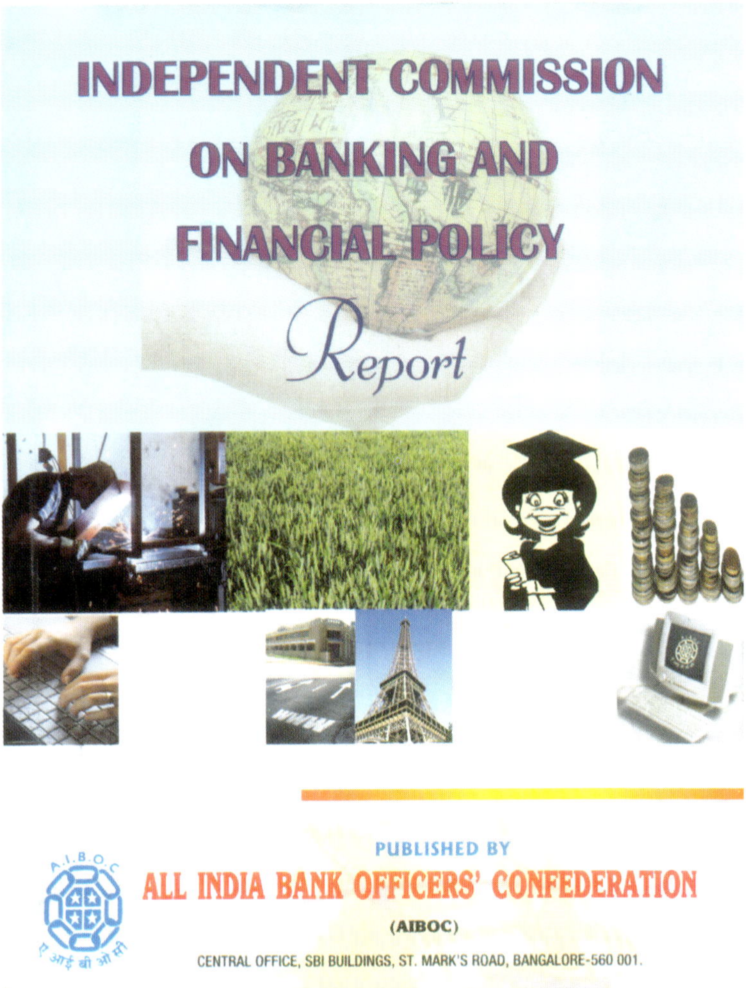
INDEPENDENT COMMISSION
ON BANKING AND
FINANCIAL POLICY
Report
A.I.B.O.C
PUBLISHED BY
ALL INDIA BANK OFFICERS' CONFEDERATION
(AIBOC)
CENTRAL OFFICE, SBI BUILDINGS, ST. MARK'S ROAD, BANGALORE-560 001.

ECONOMIC
RESEARCH
FOUNDATION
A.I.B.O.C.
INDIAN BANKING
Current Challenges & Alternatives for the Future
C. P. Chandrasekhar
Jayati Ghosh

SAVE PUBLIC SECTOR
SAVE INDIA
Parliamentary standing committee report on
NON PERFORMING ASSETS
STATE BANK OF INDIA
OFFICERS' ASSOCIATION
(Chennai Circle)

NPA IN PUBLIC SECTOR BANKS IN INDIA -
IS IT NOT A MERE TECHNICAL ISSUE?
A.I.B.O.C
ए आई बी ओ सी
All India Bank Officers' Confederation
No.84, Rajaji Salai, Chennai 600 001.

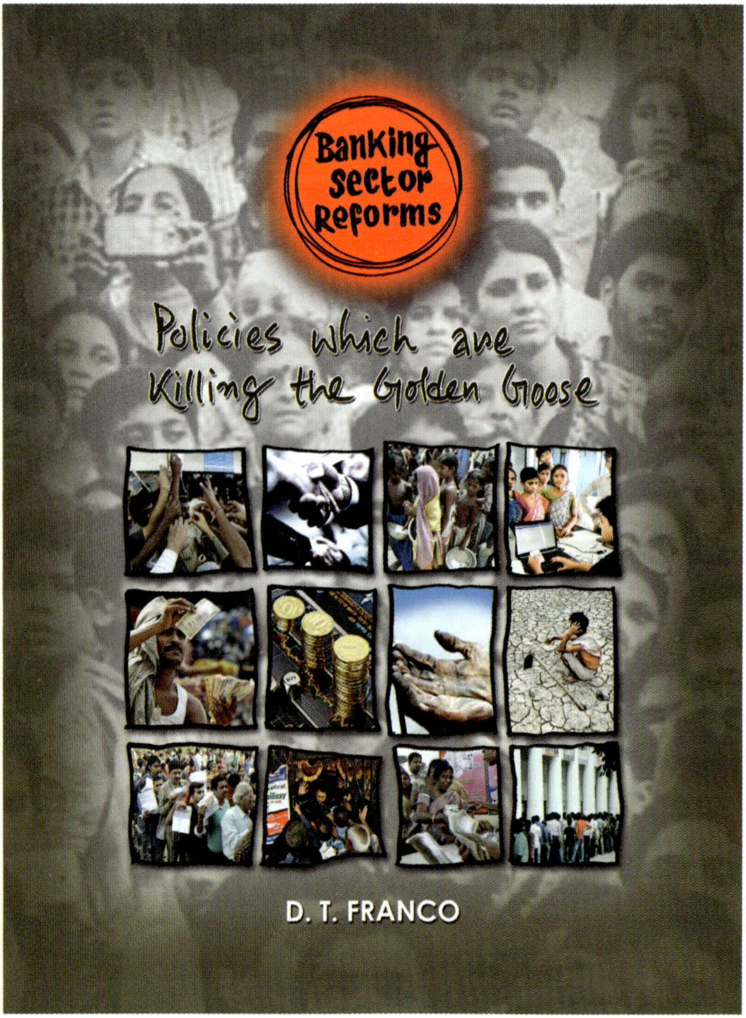
Banking Sector Reforms
Policies which are Killing the Golden Goose
D. T. FRANCO

UNITED FORUM OF BANK UNIONS
48 HOURS
CONTINUOUS BANK STRIKE
AIBOC
A.I.B.O.C
Commendable Performance of
PUBLIC SECTOR BANKS
2017-18

SAVE PUBLIC SECTOR
SAVE INDIA
Laudable Performance of
Public Sector Banks
FACTS AND LIES
ALL INDIA BANK OFFICERS' CONFEDERATION
DEMONSTRATION ON EVERY MONDAY
WE DEMAND
Appointment of board of directors representing the workmen / officers in all PSBs, immediately
Publish the list of wilful defaulters, bank wise
Reimburse the cost incurred on Demonetisation & exercise & Jan Dhan accounts
Stop moves towards merger and privatisation
Implement Parliament Standing Committee recommendations on NPA
Provide relief to farmers affected by draught.
UNITED FORUM OF BANK UNIONS
ALL INDIA BANK OFFICERS' CONFEDERATION

TURN
AROUND
PLAN FOR
ELEVEN BANKS
A.I.B.O.C
ए आई बी ओ सी
ALL INDIA BANK
OFFICERS' CONFEDERATION
SAVE PUBLIC SECTOR
SAVE INDIA

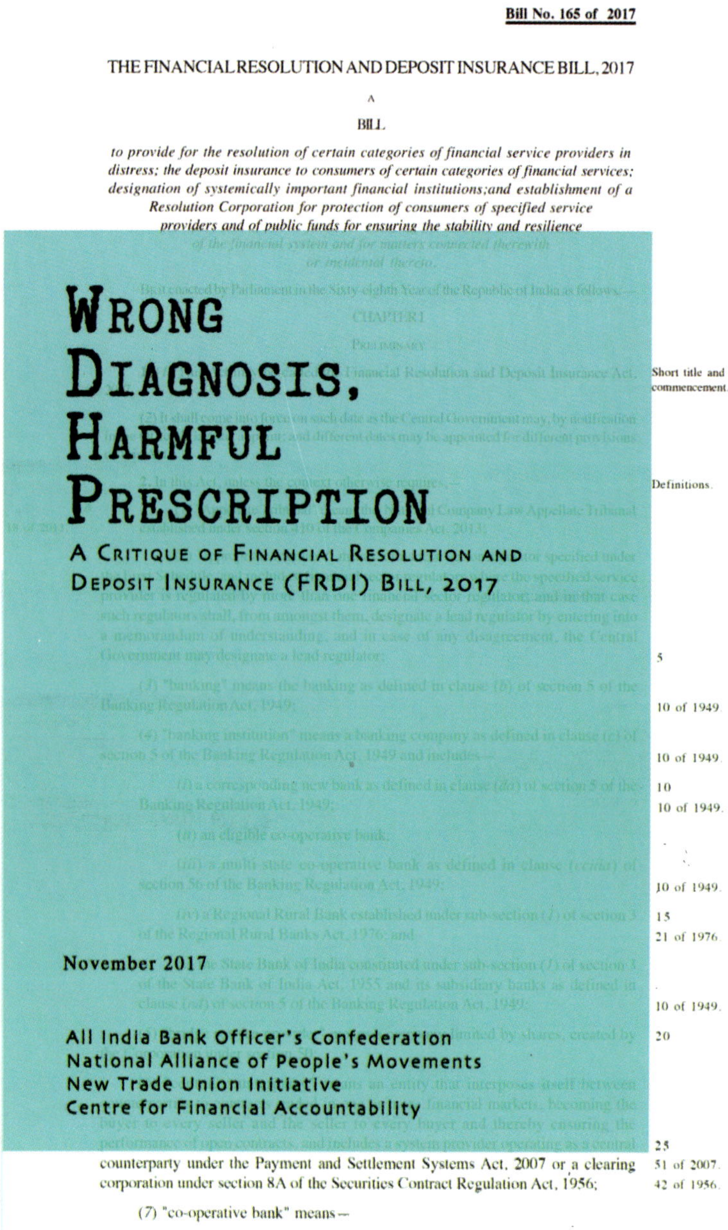

Bill No. 165 of 2017

THE FINANCIAL RESOLUTION AND DEPOSIT INSURANCE BILL, 2017

A

BILL

to provide for the resolution of certain categories of financial service providers in distress; the deposit insurance to consumers of certain categories of financial services; designation of systemically important financial institutions;and establishment of a Resolution Corporation for protection of consumers of specified service providers and of public funds for ensuring the stability and resilience

WRONG DIAGNOSIS, HARMFUL PRESCRIPTION

A CRITIQUE OF FINANCIAL RESOLUTION AND DEPOSIT INSURANCE (FRDI) BILL, 2017

November 2017

All India Bank Officer's Confederation
National Alliance of People's Movements
New Trade Union Initiative
Centre for Financial Accountability

Short title and commencement.

Definitions.

10 of 1949.

10 of 1949.

10 of 1949.

10 of 1949.

21 of 1976.

10 of 1949.

counterparty under the Payment and Settlement Systems Act, 2007 or a clearing corporation under section 8A of the Securities Contract Regulation Act, 1956; 51 of 2007. 42 of 1956.

(*7*) "co-operative bank" means—